THE
COWBOY
AND HIS
ELEPHANT

Also by Malcolm MacPherson

Protégé

The Lucifer Key

The Blood of His Servants

The Black Box

Time Bomb

In Cahoots

Deadlock

The Black Box II

THE
COWBOY
AND HIS
ELEPHANT

THE STORY OF
A REMARKABLE FRIENDSHIP

Malcolm MacPherson

HEADLINE

First published in the United States in 2001
by Thomas Dunne Books
An imprint of St Martin's Press

First published in Great Britain in 2001
by HEADLINE BOOK PUBLISHING

10 9 8 7 6 5 4 3 2 1

British Library Cataloguing in Publication Data

MacPherson, Malcolm, 1943–
    The cowboy and his elephant : the story of a
    remarkable friendship
    1.MacPherson, Malcolm
    2.Elephants - Colorado
    3.Human-animal relationships
    I.Title
    599.6'7

ISBN 0 7472 7488 6

Text design by Michelle McMillian

Printed and bound by
Mackays of Chatham plc, Chatham, Kent

HEADLINE BOOK PUBLISHING
A division of Hodder Headline
338 Euston Road
London NW1 3BH

www.headline.co.uk
www.hodderheadline.com

For the author, this boook is dedicated to

Jane Erkenbeck, with love and appreciation

And for Robert Norris, this book is also dedicated to

The autism Foundation,
My loving wife, Jane,
Our children and grandchildren,
And all animal lovers wherever they might be

There's right and there's wrong. You get to do one or the other. You do one, and you're living. You do the other, and you may be walking around, but you're as dead as a beaver hat.

— JOHN WAYNE

THE
COWBOY
AND HIS
ELEPHANT

PROLOGUE

The elephant that escapes the cull is called the Storyteller.
She tells other elephants of the good and evil that men have
done to her and her kind, and holds these truths in her
heart forever. And in the end, in summing up, her story is
taken into account. She is ancient and wise and sublime,
and her words weigh heavily in the final ledger.

Elephant hunters in Africa believe this to be true. One old
hunter, sitting at a campfire after the sun falls gives voice to
his fear. Insistence, awe, and a hint of unease tinge his voice
when he recalls, "All the years when we went for a herd we
said that *not one elephant must escape us*! If one does, we will
follow her the rest of our days. No matter what! She must
not be allowed to tell other elephants what she saw. Ele-

phants talk to each other. Yes! We know. We know if from hunting them and we have hunted them forever. Not one must ever get out alive. Listen to me! *This is true*. The Storyteller is real."

CHAPTER ONE

What the old hunter knows is legend. Among all the animals no tighter bond of emotion exists than the one between female elephants, who live with their mothers until they die. Through the ages they have wandered the plains of southern Africa in mother-daughter-grandmother "communions." They have lived *for* and *within* one another, with no conceivable distinct existence. Indeed, separation condemns them to a living death by the most painful of means—longing for the herd. Only a special few elephants have ever triumphed over this loss and loneliness. One of them was born in Zimbabwe in the spring of 1988.*

---

*The early life of this elephant, until the cull, cannot be known. This composite is drawn from numerous academic behavior studies of elephants as well as personal observations in that region of Africa.

———

A short time before her birth, in the last contractions of labor, her mother had squatted on her hind legs, her sides heaving with the weight of her burden. With a bellow and gargantuan groans and sighs she pushed the infant from her womb neck first, with its head tucked between its long forelegs, somewhat resembling a high diver. The light-gray-colored bundle dropped onto the ground with a soft thud and lay in stillness inside the clear wrapping of the amnion. Other elephants looked on, apparently with intense curiosity.

The mother let out a sigh and a shudder. She extended her trunk and helped her baby escape the sac that had been her world for the twenty-two months since her conception. The infant struggled with an instinctive urgency to steady her own ungainly legs. She slipped in the mud of mixed dirt and amniotic fluid. She raised herself again, but she did not stay upright. Drained by the effort of standing, falling, and falling again, she tried to raise herself one last time. Now her aunties, as elephant researchers sometimes call older females, rushed in to steady her. With their pointed pink trunk "fingers" they touched her body tenderly.

With that a fanfare of trumpeting, harrumphs, rumbles, and thunderous stomping and dusting—altogether a raucous celebration—filled the air. The females trumpeted and bellowed, defecated, and ran in shambling circles of pure elephants' joy.

Hearing the news from afar, relatives from the herd came

around. The bulls stood apart, throwing trunks of powder-dry ocher dust in clouds over their heads and rumbling to one another, curious and aloof. They eyed the teenage females in passing to try to judge their readiness to breed. And soon, as always, they lost interest and went back to sparring with their tusks. They posed, huge and majestic, and challenged one another with playful charges and furious dustings, squabbling over who was better than whom.

The females paid them slight heed. As they fussed over the baby, their displays of genuine caring were as heartwarming as any in nature. The birth brought them great pleasure—or whatever elephants feel when theirs is *the* world in which a baby has been born. This generosity of spirit reflected some deeper, mysterious, and unique emotion that only some few females of the mammalian species can feel. In this female world of such close community, the newborn was *theirs*, as if she had emerged from their collective elephant-family womb. The baby was their new daughter, granddaughter, cousin, and niece, but to each elephant of childbearing age, as an individual, she was also her baby alone.

And what an arrival she was! Shiny and new, tippy on her feet and nearly blinded by the sharp African light, she peeked out from between her mother's legs and uttered her first cry of "*Pra-pra*," the tiny plaint of a newborn that means "I'm hungry." Her mother gave a soothing rumble from deep within her, and rich, chalk-colored milk dripped from her nipples.

As a normal and, one might say, *beautiful* baby, the new-born stood about two and a half feet tall at the shoulders and weighed slightly under 150 pounds. She was battleship gray (bright pink behind her ears), with baggy pink skin bunched at her knees like a child in her grandpa's long underwear. The hair on her head—a frizzy, wine-colored cap—gave her a confused, sleepy look, like someone whom the inconvenience of birth had startled out of a delicious dream. Standing in the shadow of her mother's flanks, she explored her own being with a dubious mien.

She swayed her trunk as if it were a deadweight. An irritable look in her sharp brown eyes seemed to say, *This whatever it is on the front of my face is a mistake. Please, whoever gave it to me, remove it.* She had no control over the trunk's finer functions and only a modicum of command over the larger of its forty-thousand muscles. For now it was plainly a nuisance. She stepped on it with a squeak of pain. It got in the way of her mouth, suckling her mother's breasts. She slept on it under her head when she lay down. It altogether seemed to be a bother, and would remain a bafflement for some time to come.

Her map-of-Africa ears, rubbery and pinned to her head, soon flared and startled her. Their purpose too was hard for her to grasp. She could see them with her peripheral vision, and when their shadows fell on the Kalahari sands, she spooked, screamed, and ran to find her mother.

Her legs were long, thin, and unsteady. In the coming weeks she would watch the older females cross their back legs at the knees while standing in repose, and when she tried to imitate them, she would fall over on her side. Her legs commanded her in directions she did not wish to go, like someone at the mercy of strong gusts of wind.

Her broad forelegs were like cumbersome round winter boots encasing the dainty feet of a ballerina *on pointe*. She could feel herself walking gracefully on tiptoes, but when she looked down she saw only tree stumps. She could not even glimpse her tail, which hung down from the end of her ridged spine like a short hemp strand with a frizzy, blown-apart tip that resembled nothing so much as an exploded trick cigar. Neither could she see around her bowed sides how the skin under her tail and around her back thighs drooped like oversize trousers slipping down to her knees.

As a whole, if her mother or her aunties had whispered to her in those first hours after her birth that God had drawn her as a silly cartoon, she would have had to agree. She possessed no sleekness, no aerodynamics, no impression of grace or speed or agility.

Though her mother, as a young adult, had grown into her mature elephant proportions, she, like all elephants, would continue to expand in size and weight throughout her life. She towered over her baby. Nine feet tall at her shoulders and weighing 4,400 pounds, she gave scale to the baby's tiny size and weight. She was the image of what the baby would grow up to be over a long period of physical maturation that parallels the stages of human development.

For now, infancy exposed in stark relief the baby's parts: Nothing born should have had such big ears, and a nose like a hose, and such size and girth, and a tail that was hardly worthy of the name. The baby was smaller than most. Ultimately her size might shape her character: She could grow up as a runt or, by compensating for her size with intelligence and a capacity to adapt, she could become a leader. It was too soon to tell.

But Amy—as she would later come to be called—*was* already different. Her brownish, amber-colored eyes contained none of the hard darkness of the bulls or the more common dark reddish-black of other females. It was a color said to signify intelligence. Her eyes peered out of her head as if they belonged to another creature inside her baggy skin. Her baffled gaze posed the same enigma that the older female elephants raised when they would pause in unison to look skyward as a cloud floated by. According to the wise old Brahman priests in India, elephants were gods who worshiped the sun and the moon.

Amy's mother soon grew impatient and took herself several yards from the birth celebration for food and rest. A daughter of the matriarch, she was acknowledged to possess strength and character. She was smaller but more dominant than her sisters, whom she bossed, and they obeyed as if she herself were the matriarch.

Like all female elephants of every age, she switched

effortlessly from watchful mother to distracted child. Lessons for life were surely to be learned in "play," but as the true kings and queens of Africa, elephants lorded over life. They seemed to have *leisure*, which they used for friendship and gaiety, courtship, reverence—and for itself alone.

Now Amy's grandmother scooted away the aunties and cousins as if in weary disgust. Their doting over Amy threatened to weaken the baby, whose ability to keep up with the herd was a matter of her survival. The family was migrating in loose association with its herd along the western edge of their territory, inside the 423,000-acre Charisa (in the Sengwa Wildlife Research Area), on the boundary of Zimbabwe's Chizarira National Park. The Sengwa River traversed the Charisa and meandered across a valley floor of escarpments and cliffs of Karoo sandstone before pouring into Lake Kariba, some fifty miles below the falls. Each family member needed sixty pounds of forage daily to satisfy his or her appetite. Wander for food was what elephants did, how they lived, and what consumed their time. It was their *job*.

After the hiatus of the birth, the matriarch rumbled a familiar call, "*Grah*," the "Let's go" signal. The elephants stood still, as if frozen in place. They listened to her calls, and they obeyed her without question. For she alone was their link to the lore of their collective past. She was their leader. Without her they would not know what to think, or do, or where to go. Until the day she died, she was their mother, their compass, their memory.

With their ears flared, the family set off in single file at a pace to ease the strain on the baby. The aunties guarded the column's rear and flanks against the jackals and hyenas that had already devoured Amy's placenta and sought her out eagerly as a tender meal. Her mother urged her along when she scampered through a forest of legs. Many big eyes peered down and never lost sight of her. Elephants' eyes, with the acuity to spy a tiny morsel on the ground from seven or eight feet high, and to see to their sides—and with a slight movement of their head to their rear—missed nothing, especially not a 150-pound baby careening through their legs.

No sight could convince an observer of the goodness of their being more than that of female elephants on the march. They showed toward one another what humans would call contentment, joy, and affection. They touched as though they would rather have been there and nowhere else, and with no other creatures. They were at peace. Their world pleased them, as the ladies of the land. They *were* the world.

The baby Amy grew stronger, heavier, taller; and with a widening world, she was learning where she belonged in an order that changed over the seasons by birth, maturity, and death.

The elephants displayed personalities as varied as any extended human family. Unlike the bulls, who separated from the family when they reached adolescence—in their early to middle teens—and achieved their prominence through physical strength, females found their order through assertiveness, character, intelligence, and judgment; the capacity for memory, and something else mysterious and hard to define. Some elephants remained adolescents their whole lives, forgetful and foolish, while others brooded and stood aloof, and still others sought neither high nor low ground but were content to eat, breed, raise their young, remain a part of the female family, and die.

The more assertive females stood up to the younger bulls that pestered those females who had already chosen as a mate a more dominant male. These females tolerated no bullying. They stood between their sisters and trouble, and led them away from harm. They worked and lived together as a unit, subsuming individuality, while the males distinguished themselves in more clearly obvious ways, presenting themselves in broad strokes. They were cranky, or outright mean, or sometimes just timid, souls who were terrified of their own shadows, and so on. Males needed to define themselves thus. Females did not. And this made them who they were.

As a collective of mothers and mothers-to-be, the females spoiled the babies; watched over them; and nurtured, encouraged, and praised them. They did not discipline or punish them for their mistakes. A moment's inattention or a baby's wandering away from the herd to play could mean a life ended quickly. Indeed, the brutality of nature served elephants as discipline served humans.

Those who know elephants, work with them, study them, and have hunted them have never doubted their intelligence. One hunter says, "These are special animals. I know it. I'm not a guy who has ever done research. I just kept my eyes open and lived here among them for forty years. They are the most intelligent animals of all, period."

Amy depended on her elders' intelligence in times of trouble. All elephants got stuck—in mud, in pits, in bowls under the surface of shallow water, in sand. Amy was no different, *and* she was curious. Once she found herself trapped on a shelf in the river. She could not climb the bank. She screamed her alarm call. Her mother panicked and ran to her rescue. She saw the trouble, and she called the aunties to help her. With patient but insistent coordination, the adults waded into the river and pushed and prodded with their tusks and trunks to lift her up to safety.

Years before Amy's birth, when lightning had sparked a wildfire that burned hot and fast, one elephant in the family was seriously scorched, and in her agony she lost the will to flee from the flames. She screamed in pain; she faltered. The other females, heedless of their own safety, rushed into the fire and pushed her to get her out. Her family would not allow her to give up, and she lived.

Another time, also before Amy's birth, a younger female died of unknown causes. She had not been shot, and she was too young to have died of any ailment of old age. The other females, by their subsequent actions, did not believe that she was dead. They tried to pick her up. They pushed her huge body more than fifty yards into a clump of thick underbrush, where they inspected her all over with their trunks. They pushed at her; they mounted her; they screamed at her, shaded her, and brought her water.

Some hours went by. Humans arrived, and the elephants fled. The humans removed the dead elephant's tusks, and with butcher knives they cut a large panel of valuable hide off her side, leaving a broad square of bright white subcutaneous tissue exposed to the light. The females returned that night. Clearly upset by what they saw, they set out to "doctor" her. One by one they went down to the riverbank some miles distant and picked up mud, with which they returned to salve the dead elephant's whitened side. And when they were done, and the dead elephant was dark skinned once more, in the eyes of the other elephants she should have been ready to come along with them. They waited. In the morning, when she did not get up, they went on reluctantly without her.

This remarkable ability to feel distress in their own kind—and also in other, unrelated species—and to try to relieve it sets elephants apart from other species. This compassionate quality certainly impressed Alexander the Great, who fought the Battle of Hydaspes in early summer 326 B.C., in which the Indian monarch Porus was grievously wounded and would have died if the elephant he was riding had not carried him off the field of battle, laid him down on the earth, and with its trunk plucked out the arrows from his body with a gentleness that Alexander described as "human." So impressed was he that later he minted a coin in the elephant's honor.

Since then, throughout history, the compassion of elephants has intrigued, mystified, and forced on humans a reappraisal of anthropomorphism as a needless and artificial wall between humans and other animals. For the most part women anthropologists (Cynthia Moss, Joyce Poole, Katy Payne, Daphne Sheldrick, and others) have pioneered this sensible, logical view through their studies of elephants, using words like "fun," "silly," "sad," and "happy" to describe aspects of elephant behavior. Sheldrick, for one, says, "[Elephants] have a sense . . . that projects beyond their own kind and sometimes extends to others in distress. They help one another in adversity, miss an absent loved one, and when you know them really well, you can see that they even smile when [they are] having fun and are happy."

A measure of elephants' intelligence is their ability to communicate over long distances through sound frequencies below the level of human hearing. Elephant researchers such as Katy Payne have recorded the sounds of elephants, which some skeptics have dismissed as noise. But the debate over meaning would seem silly to a child, who might reasonably ask, *If elephants don't talk over such long distances, why do they have such big ears?* In fact these function as biological radiators to cool the blood to an elephant's brain. But is that all? Might not the same ears also scoop delicate low-frequency bundles of sound (messages) out of the air, just as humans' huge parabolic radio telescopes sweep the skies for scintillas of celestial sound (messages)? Why do some think of one as ridiculous when the other is called science?

There is no doubt that elephants' sounds had shaken the air above the Sengwa with a warning to Amy's family, then browsing along a southward track within the Lake Kariba watershed, and within the boundaries of the research area. In response the family had shifted farther west. From time to time the older females lifted their trunks high above their heads, sweeping the air for the scent of danger. For verification the matriarch hoisted the end of another female's trunk as if to say, I *smell danger. Do you?* She acted as if she did not know how to decide. The patterns of the sounds were mixed, and the smells seemed vague. There might be danger ahead, but it had neither a shape nor an identity that the family could understand. And the matriarch relied on the patterns, customs, routes, and rituals that had protected her family before. These new warnings were frightening—without content. For several weeks, while the herd's bulls continued on their southward migration, the females slowed down and listened, and waited until there was silence again.

The whole world of Amy's family had not changed for generations, until about fifty years ago, when humans began to farm the lands that were the elephants' traditional migration grounds. The products of human toil and the sun and the rain, the crops were seen by the elephants simply as glorious gifts. The consequences of this misunderstanding would soon spark a tragic chain of events that would change baby Amy's life forever.

For now she was learning to become self-sufficient. She still nursed at her mother's breasts, but as she grew and gained weight, she needed occasional food supplements. She watched the adults strip the bark from trees, reach for the higher branches and pull them down, lean into trees with their broad rumps and foreheads and shove them down, pound the dirt bulbs off grasses, and snap the stiff fronds of palms with their tusks. The sound and commotion of their foraging could be heard for a hundred yards.

More than anything else the elephants in Amy's family— like all African elephants—were eating machines with pass-through digestive tracts that absorbed only a fraction of their foods' nutrition. They needed plenty to get by. And so they cleared the vegetation in their path, almost as though a war had recently been fought there. They did not know the meaning of sharing, and left very little for other animal species that browsed after them. They needed vast tracts of fodder to keep them alive, while every other species down the food chain had to settle for what was left.

As weeks followed the days after her birth, Amy's world

widened to include her cousins. They roughhoused and heaped up their bodies in elephantine "pig piles" with trumpets of glee. They rammed one another and butted, collided, and rolled over on each other. Play satisfied their need for intimacy through touch. Amy assessed her cousins as individuals with strengths and weaknesses. She was quick to grasp the pecking order. She was growing up to become even-tempered, somewhat aloof, and mature for her age.

Her older cousins had taught her by example to pull her mother's tail, ears, and trunk. Sometimes when she was tired she leaned against her mother's leg as if it were a convenient pillar. She touched all over her mother's body and stroked her mother's velvety tongue with the fingers of her trunk. In those intimate moments her eyes closed dreamily, and she purred with what seemed like utter contentment.

Her personality began to develop. For one thing, she was even more than normally reluctant to share. She stole food out of other elephants' mouths with daring and stealth, with which she compensated for her smaller size. She distracted her cousins, then scooped their food into her mouth and walked away as if nothing had happened. She chased and skirmished with zebras, which fled and then stopped, turned, and stared at her. Baboons charged her with loud coughing cries. A plover no bigger than a human's hand, refusing to fly, its feet planted on the dried mud near a wallow and its feathers puffed up, chased Amy away with its strident calls. The wind in the trees, the shadows of clouds on the ground, falling leaves, crawling insects and reptiles, "ghosts" and imagined creatures—almost anything served to give Amy the thrill of fear. Butterflies dancing on the air in balloons of color sent her running, while the older females watched them flutter past with the appreciation of bystanders at a parade.

Like all young elephants Amy loved the frisson of being chased. In mock terror she trumpeted and shot her trunk straight out in front of her like a lance, with which she parted the high grass as she fled. Out of breath, she turned around and seeing how far she had separated herself from the others, ran in real terror to rejoin them. And when they met and were together again, her limbs, shoulders, and ears went floppy and loose. She shook her head as if in elephant laughter, while the mothers and aunties, standing in the shade of the leafy *mopanes*, watched and rumbled and nodded as if they approved.

The whole family played in the wallow—any shallow pan of water mixed with dirt or any riverbank or any watering hole. Glorious mud was all that was needed. On hot days the mud soothed skin that was neither thick nor coarse. To rid themselves of a mosquito, fly, or bee the elephants gyrated, leaped, rolled, ran, and crashed into mud with bellows that sounded very much like those of relief. (If hunger did not take them away constantly in search of food, elephants would probably bathe all day, every day.) A bath in the early afternoon suited Amy's family, and another in the evening. A long drink in the morning and a splash and wade gave the day its start. Water was a luxury as precious as new life to elephants. At its sight, or its scent nearby, they trumpeted and bellowed, and the younger elephants raced ahead and crashed in up to their knees, headless of what creatures had arrived before them. The older females held back, drank and pounded holes in the mudbank with their heels, and splashed mud over their backs and bellies, waiting until the youngsters were ready to eat again.

At the river's edge Amy timidly rolled over in a slippery bowl of muddy water. It was cool and smelled musty, of decayed vegetation. Her skin glistened with slick mud. It was a world she clearly wished never to leave. But soon she was ready to feed, and when she tried to stand up, her legs slipped, and she fell and slid to the bottom of the pan. With a complete loss of dignity, she finally crawled out and ran to her mother for reassurance.

The older elephants stayed in the middle of the river and filled their stomachs with enough water to overcome their natural buoyancy. They walked along the bottom as hippos do, breathing through trunks held aloft like snorkels. Trunks waved above the water like black snakes on glass.

The teenage elephants bathed somewhat closer to the riverbank. They held their heads above the water, braided their trunks in twos and threes, and bobbed like huge black corks. In this weightless world they danced impromptu ballets with sinewy grace. They swam by instinct and could cover great distances in water when the need arose. One family was once observed swimming one hundred miles without a rest, the stronger females giving the weaker ones a lift with their trunks. Their matriarch, it seemed, had led her family on a migration route that had been flooded in the family's long absence by the construction of the Kariba Dam and the subsequent formation of the artificial Lake Kariba.

Amy—now in her tenth month—still needed her mother to nurture her, but she was found more and more in the company of the family's other females, the aunties and older cousins and sisters, who raised her, protected her, taught her, and played with her. On tree-shaded riverbanks Amy looked at her aunties as if to say, *Now this would be a good place for me to roll over, and maybe you could tickle me.*

All elephants clearly loved being tickled, no matter what their ages. Amy was as ticklish as any child. Even the old matriarch enjoyed a tickle now and then. Quick to find playmates, Amy rolled in the grass and split the air with trumpeting sounds of elephant laughter as older cousins played the fingers of their trunks down her ribs and in her armpits and the soft crannies under her chin. At these times the family could lose sight of one another, discovering with a sudden fright that they were being left behind, and they caught up to the other elephants in a hurry.

When the family met its bond group—the elephants with whom they shared common ancestors—the reunions were extravagant displays of pure elephant emotion. As they came within sight and sound of one another, the families ran and touched and stomped and defecated and twined trunks and bumped foreheads and dusted and clicked

ivories. It did not seem to matter if they had met and celebrated like this only an hour before. Elephants could never
say hello too often.

Their dead were greeted with a show of respect. When they
came upon the bones of a blood relative, they always lin-
gered to caress the bones with their trunks. Did they plan
their route to intersect with the graves of their fallen family
members? Amy watched her mother touch a sun-bleached
elephant skull on the ground. She snaked her trunk in the
eyehole and brushed over its surface, almost as though she
were grieving for the dead relative, remembering her in life.

Even at her young age, Amy rolled the bones and picked
them up and dropped them with a different, even solemn,
behavior.

Now almost a year had gone by. After plentiful spring
rains, Amy's family was reminded of the fields at the bottom
of their migration route. Last season while the bulls had
eaten the crops of the humans, the females stood at the
boundary fence without daring to cross into the forbidden
territory. Perhaps this year would be different, and they
would feast in the cornfields too.

As time went by, Amy was adding one hundred pounds to
her weight every couple of months. Everything was happening faster now. She had to use her trunk with greater dexter-
ity to feed herself the foods that she saw her aunties and

cousins eat. Sometimes a bouquet of green grass grasped in her trunk ended on the top of her head or draped over her ears. At other times she snatched a leaf or grass directly from her mother's mouth. Eating on her own, she identified the grass by sniffing it: then she pulled it up or broke it off, and brought it up to her mouth and ground it with her molars.

Drinking frustrated her. Water was hard to hold. She siphoned it into her trunk by breathing in, but *not* inhaling too hard lest the water go to her head. Then she would sneeze loudly, spraying the air with a fine mist. She practiced sucking water up in her trunk. She learned to raise her head and reach the tip of her trunk up to her lips. The older elephants, who drank without effort, forced the water into their mouths by gently blowing. Amy let gravity work for her. The water drained out of her trunk and dribbled into her mouth. And as she repeated this exercise, she gained proficiency and could be said to drink on her own.

She was rapidly acquiring social skills as well. Again, as in everything else, she learned by observation, example, and trial and error. She noticed those males in the herd that from time to time came around to check for females in estrous. In comparison to her family members, these males were huge and overbearing, their behavior direct and single-minded. The presence of the males intrigued all the family's females, no matter what their ages. By watching her aunties and older cousins with the males, Amy learned lessons for use later in life.

She was communicating with her family more often now, learning the basic elephant language by listening and entering the "discussions." And from the leadership of the matriarch she was gaining useful knowledge of her habitat. Indeed, she was reaching a time when she would start to show the other elephants what she was to become—strong, resourceful, and prepared to contribute in important ways to the family's future.

Then more time passed, and the females finally approached the boundary of their reserve. The whole herd at last was together again. As the sun set, the air around the southern edge of the Sengwa filled with elephant sounds. The long-awaited feast was soon to begin. This was the moment they had all waited for. Majestic and sublime, they were the greatest creatures to walk the land.

The headman of the Tonga, a skinny old great-grandfather with crooked teeth, was the enemy of the elephants. He hated them. *Vermin*, Siwelo Bvathlomoy Dingani said. *No better than rats!*

At that moment Dingani was leaning on the gnarled stick that he used as a cane. Even this early in the morning Dingani despaired as he limped past the village's cinder block shed, where the corn was ground into meal. Its gas engine had lain idle for days with nothing to mill from the fields. Roosters crowed, the hens scratched the dirt, and a black pig burrowed its nose into a heap of garbage. Villagers emerged from their thatch-roofed huts for the first time since sundown. Out early before school began, Dingani's great-grandsons started to play a game of soccer in the dirt lot in back of the huts, kicking an object that rolled but was not an inflatable ball.

Dingani did not have to walk far to come within view of the southern edge of the Sengwa Wildlife Research Area. He saw the fence that was supposed to keep the elephants out of the village's cropland. Then he turned to look at that land. The evidence of the elephants' damage from the previous night was strewn everywhere. Soon nothing would be left of the spring planting.

Necessity had taught the Tonga tribe, which numbered around a million, how to survive. As refugees in a foreign land, they were ignored by Zimbabwe's ruling tribe. Forty years earlier colonial Britain had forced the Tonga on Zimbabwe (then Southern Rhodesia) to make way for the opening of the Kariba Dam. Poor soil since then had given them paltry, bitter harvests. And now the elephants had the same devastating effect on their crops as any flood or plague of locusts.

The sight of the cornstalks in the fields had emboldened the elephants behind the fence. They lined up each evening, waiting for the sun to set. A fence, even the elephants knew, was only as good as its repair, and nights ago the stronger bulls had pushed a younger one into the electrified wire, sparks flew, the circuit shorted out, and the fence had been worthless as an elephant barrier ever since. Most nights the elephants stepped out of their reserve onto the lands adjacent to Dingani's village. Afraid to go out of their huts, the villagers listened to the feasting in their maize fields. At sunrise the raiders were gone again, and so too were several acres of the Tonga's precious crops.

Dingani had no idea what to do to save his people. The law forbade Tonga ownership of guns. Hunting with any kind of weapon was proscribed. Dingani had asked the officers in the Game Department for help. The last he had heard from them, they were ending their system of elephant control. With it would go the village's last hope of salvation.

In the den of his split-level farmhouse in Zimbabwe's Gwayi Valley, a white African rancher, Buck deVries, hung up the telephone. He walked into the dining room, where his family, already seated at the dinner table, waited for him to say the blessing. They held hands in a circle and bowed their heads, and in his native Afrikaans, deVries uttered thanks to God. As they passed around a tureen of steaming kudu stew, deVries turned to his wife, Rita. "They've just told me the Tonga have asked the Zimbabwe government for another cull"—a slaughter of all those elephants that had encroached on tribal lands—he told her, and mentioned where. He also told her it was going to be the last one.

Rita deVries knew all too well that her husband had a secret commitment to keep.

A superstitious sixty-eight-year-old, deVries had vowed long ago to rescue at least one elephant from the slaughter. Perhaps as a hunter, his commitment to this rescue was meant to atone for a lifetime of taking elephants' lives, necessary as he believed that to be. He was to be a rescuer, not a savior. He could not release any elephant he was going to save back into the wild, or raise her to adulthood, or even keep her on his ranch for long. Sure, he could use the money (four thousand American dollars) an exotic animal broker would pay him for her. He had misgivings about that, but, knowing what he knew, anyplace would be better for this young elephant than the continent of her birth.

"Why, Mother, is this a good place for her to stay," he asked his wife, "if she needs me to rescue her from the guns?"

DeVries wanted to leave Africa himself if he could, with his whole family. The bitterness, the war, the intertribal killings, the feeling of being unwanted, the politics—these had turned this beautiful country into a living nightmare for its white settlers.

Buck knew that rescue meant more than saving a baby elephant for a day or from a single cull. It meant for as long as the elephant lived. Zimbabwe was a dangerous place for an elephant, with systematic culls almost certain to be revived again sometime in the future, with the poaching of elephants for their ivory tusks, with a lack of food for man and beast, and with the shootings of elephants by some tribesmen bent on their eradication. What lay ahead for Zimbabwe's elephants was anyone's guess. The elephant he would save would need an ultimate savior, someone other than himself to watch over her. But someone had to make the first effort, and Buck was as close to the front lines of elephant survival as anyone could be.

Two days after deVries was told about the cull, a convoy of twelve Game Department diesel trucks rumbled through the morning mist carrying at least fifty Africans in shorts, overalls, and sweaters of forest green. Guns wrapped in soft blankets lay under seats. On their hemp belts the men carried scabbards made of elephant tails, which held sharpening steels. Around their necks they tied kerchiefs to cover their mouths and noses against the stench of death.

DeVries bounced along through the dust at the end of the convoy in his Ford pickup, which he had customized with wooden sides and an awning over the truck bed. His kidneys ached, and his back throbbed from the jolting ride over the open terrain of the research area. Alone with his thoughts, he reflected on what his oldest son, Johannes Jacobus deVries, would have been like now. Buck missed him dearly; he and Rita had called the boy Zoon. Big for his age, he had worn an adult shoe when he was only twelve. Zoon loved to hunt springboks and fish for tilapia and tigerfish. One day shortly after his twelfth birthday, while he was out angling alone on the brush-cluttered banks of the Zambezi River, Zoon was attacked by a large crocodile that suddenly rose out of the murky waters and killed him. Some twenty years later, age and time had cooled Buck's rage over this terrible death as they sustained the grief over his loss.

Now the sight of a light airplane flying over the convoy

distracted him from his thoughts. The evening before, the airplane had crossed the area to locate the elephant herds; it had returned to assist in the cull.

A few miles on, the convoy pulled to the side of the road in a defile near a stand of *moupane* trees. Sometimes called the Dark Continent, Africa was more the Silent Continent, and this morning it was no different. The men disembarked from the trucks without a sound, their boots and shoes sinking into the sandy Kalahari soil.

Suddenly the noise of the airplane engine broke the stillness, and two-way radios crackled with static. The pilot revved the engine and banked over the treetops in tight circles. He had sighted the elephant herd and was "pushing" them toward the hunters, who were just then loading their guns.

The elephants of Amy's family—adult cows, adolescents, and Amy—screamed, trumpeted, and bellowed at the horrible sound of the airplane. They ran behind their matriarch, trying to get away, until they came upon the men who faced them with guns aimed. The elephants stopped. The airplane seemed to be everywhere at once—above, behind them and at their sides. In front of them stood the men. There was nowhere to turn. Then the shooting started, the guns exploding in unison. The first elephant killed by gunfire, the matriarch of Amy's family, slumped on her front knees, then fell over dead on her side. Amid the racket of the airplane and the exploding guns, Amy's mother and several other older females in the family rushed to where the matriarch lay dead.

They touched and pushed her, trying to help her get up. Her death was inconceivable to them, and their pitiful attempt to save her, refusing to leave her, spelled their quick doom.

Now without her they did not know what to do or where to go. They had no leader. Out of fear they screamed, bellowed, and defecated. They trumpeted to locate the young elephants that were scattering in panic. The older females formed their bodies into a tight phalanx in front of the matriarch. The guns fired nearly point-blank, and the elephants' powerful legs went out from under them as if the earth had swallowed them up. They fell on top of one another. One shooter climbed onto a dead elephant and shot from that vantage point. Men were shouting. Amy stayed near her mother; then her mother was shot. Amy tried to burrow her head under her mother's chin.

"That one! That one!" a voice cried. "Do *not* shoot that one!"

Hands pulled Amy away from her mother's body, though she tried to run away. The gunfire was ending. She struggled out of their grasp. Men with ropes chased her and jumped on her back and straddled her. She was exhausted, terrified, and confused. Men's hands forced her ears over her eyes. A thin rope went around her head. She was blinded. She could hear the dying sighs and groans of her family. She could smell their deaths. Her family had been slaughtered! Then there was a sharp prick on the inside of one ear, and in an instant, everything slipped away.

DeVries worked fast. He moistened Amy's eyes with drops. He listened closely to her breathing. He ordered several men nearby to help him pull her over to his truck. Fifteen minutes went by. The guns were stacked out of sight. Then, "All of a sudden everyone else let go of the baby and ran away," deVries remembered. "Amazingly, her mother was up! Although she was shot, she was not dead. It was like she had come back to life at the sight of what was happening to her baby and was charging us at full speed. I stayed with the baby; I did not run with the others. The mother went right past me to reach the men who were running away. She caught two of them and knocked one flat out on the ground. The other one fell under her tusks. The one between her legs tried to crawl out the back way on his hands and knees. She did not make a sound. She pushed him forward with her back legs. She would not let him get away. She was standing on her knees. She wrapped her trunk around him. She was stabbing at him with her tusks. His pants were torn off, and his shirt was torn off, and he was screaming. The other man was still trying to get away.

"One of the hunters ran to find his rifle. He came back. He aimed. *Pkaaaa!*" Amy's mother was dead.

In the silence that followed, the Africans slipped their sharpening steels out of their scabbards. They slid butchering knives up and down the steels with a buzzing of blades.

DeVries injected Amy's ear with an antidote to the Scoline tranquilizer. She struggled to her feet and cried out. No call from her family came in reply. She pushed her trunk out a narrow slit in the truck's gate, searching for the scents of her mother, her aunties, and cousins. She screamed for an hour as the truck made its way slowly out of the bush in the direction of the nearest dirt road. From time to time deVries stopped to give her water and fresh leafy branches that he slashed off trees with a machete.

Later the sun set and the twilight passed swiftly; then it was dark. The Ford's headlights jittered and picked out darkened silhouettes against a line of *moupane* and Rhodesian mahogany trees. At first deVries could not distinguish the shapes. Amy cried out. The dark shadows moved across the truck's beams. A whole new family of female elephants was running straight at his truck. DeVries remembers, "I was being ambushed. Oh, yes, my friend, it happened. I turned off the truck lights. These elephants pushed the truck backward and forward. The baby cried. The elephants made a helluva noise. I was frightened. I put the truck in third gear and moved forward slowly. I could feel the elephants hit the truck with their bodies. They were trying to turn it over. The whole family of elephants pushed right up against the truck. They tried like hell to get the baby out, I swear to you. I thought I should let her go. I would have been killed if I had tried to get out of the truck. I moved away, I don't know how far. I turned on the lights. The elephants were gone. What had happened there that night was very strange."

An adult bull elephant deVries had found long ago as an orphaned baby and raised as a pet, was waiting for Amy in the pen that night when deVries drove up the road to his ranch house. He had rescued the bull, whom he named Jumbo, by the Gwayi River, in a mud wallow that he could not get out of. "Growing up, Jumbo had a milk cow for his mother," deVries recalled. "When the cow lay down Jumbo lay down right next to her. You could hear him snore a mile away. He was afraid that she would leave him; he laid his trunk over her stomach, and when she got up he woke up and followed her. The cow knew that Jumbo was not her calf. He got bigger and bigger. But she didn't seem to mind."

Released from the back of deVries's truck, Amy ran to Jumbo—one orphan to another—at the far end of a corral made of wide sheets of rubber conveyor belt salvaged from a coal mine. All through that first night and for several nights thereafter, even with Jumbo by her side, Amy's long, high-pitched screams kept Rita deVries awake. When daylight dawned, Amy was standing by the bull elephant and would not move from his side. DeVries set out a radio with the volume low to calm her. He wanted her to hear people talking, and the sound of music. As deVries understood her future, she was going to be among humans for the rest of her life, and he wanted to help her understand their ways.

32

A young animal cast into a strange world for which she was wholly unprepared, she had to learn how to be an orphan. Though she was partly weaned, she could not survive on solid foods alone. Rita deVries worked out a formula of boiled rice mixed with powdered milk that she warmed on her kitchen woodstove. Rita helped Amy eat. She sat on a stool in front of her pen and placed her trunk in the bucket of milk, which Amy sucked up. She had to learn the harder task of transferring the milk from the bucket to her mouth, and that was where Rita helped. With the milk in Amy's trunk, Rita guided the end of her trunk into her mouth. After a while Amy learned to suck the milk into her mouth as if through a straw. Then Rita put Amy's trunk back in the bucket for another sip, repeating the procedure over and over. Because the milk stayed fresh in the African heat only for an hour, Rita would go back to the house to prepare more. Amy drank a cup of milk every ten minutes or so, twenty-four hours a day. Rita deVries remembers, "Eventually she decided if she sucked a little bit she could hold it in her trunk by herself. She could get the milk out herself. At first she blew it all over her face, but in three or four days she got it right, and then she sucked a little bit and blew it into her mouth. She was feeding herself. At that stage we had every hope that at least she would survive."

The nights were cold, and deVries burned logs down to coals, which he shoveled against the cinder block wall outside Amy's pen. She pressed her body against the inside of the thick wall and absorbed its comforting warmth. In the mornings she walked around the *kraal*, or pen. She joined Jumbo, and from her place by his side she looked out at her new world. Hens clucked and roosters crowed; the deVries family's Rhodesian Ridgebacks growled and barked. A pet lion that Rita had raised from a cub stalked the fence. Cars, trucks, and tractors drove by, blowing black diesel smoke from their exhausts. Most of the time Amy stayed close to Jumbo, shivering with fright.

Removed from familiar sights, sounds, and smells—and roped, yanked, and prodded—the young elephant was on her way to becoming a commodity worth her value as a "curiosity" to humans, probably far away from Africa, as an attraction in a European zoo. Just then she needed kindness and love as much as food and water to live. Now that the bond of female elephant emotion had been broken, Amy must have felt lost. Her whole world had disappeared with the death of her cousins and aunties, her mother and the matriarch. She was alone, yet she was alive.

In the next months Amy was trained to accept being enclosed in a wooden crate, in which she ate and slept. She could not have known why she was made to enter the crate day after day, but she grew accustomed to it. She was learning to survive. New sounds bothered her, but less so than at first. Strange new sights were frightening, but she no longer automatically ran to the safety of Jumbo's side.

One day a man she had not seen before came to the edge of the pen and leaned over to look at her. He talked with deVries, then walked back to the house. The stranger was a broker of exotic African animals who was buying Amy and would sell her to a circus or a zoo somewhere in the world. Her future was decided.

On the day of her departure deVries went to say good-bye. In his hand he carried a stick of chalk. He felt that he had satisfied his commitment by helping one elephant to escape the cull. Now she had to move on, but he could not let her go away nameless. In bold letters he wrote on the side of her crate: AMY, with the hope that anyone who met her, wherever she was bound, would recognize the word to mean "friend."

She flew out of Africa with five other baby elephants. After the Boeing 747 lifted off from Johannesburg's Jan Smuts Airport, the Lufthansa captain announced to the people flying with him, "Listen, we have some unusual passengers with us today."

The flight attendants visited the baby elephants in the airplane's rear cargo compartment. The crew adjusted the temperature for their comfort. A keeper watched over them, perched on top of a crate, talking to them. He used the Swahili word for elephant. "*Tembos*, quiet. *Tembos*, quiet," he said.

CHAPTER TWO

B
ob Norris tilted his hat and gazed over the land that men like him had roamed for a century and more. In the wind he heard the echoes of the stories that cowboys on cattle drives told around campfires, of longhorns and of their beloved ponies. His reverie was broken by one of his ranch hands, who had come up to have a word with him.

The two men were standing outside in the cool Colorado air, in front of the gallery of the ranch's horse barn. The snowy peaks of the Rockies shone like fiery beacons in the eastern light. Between the ranch and the Rockies rolled the green hills of the Front Range. The cowboy's horse-and-cattle ranch spread south and west from where he was standing, farther than the eye could see.

The ranch hand, named Don, reported, "Some guy came

over here earlier this morning. Said he wanted to rent a couple of stalls. I told him to get out of here. We don't do that."

"That was diplomatic," Bob said ironically. A small grin wrinkled his handsome face.

"He's comin' back to talk to you this afternoon."

"That's fine," Bob said. "What's he need the stalls for?"

"He wouldn't say."

"Well, hell, for a horse or kangaroos or what?"

"Horses, I guess," said Don uncertainly.

Bob let it go for the moment. He had chores to do. And besides, with the welcome he had received from Don, he doubted that the stranger would come back soon. He went in the barn for a ladder, which he carried over to the grain silo. He climbed up to the steel rungs set into the concrete, and then up to a dizzying height. He straddled the silo's rim as if it were a horse. A truck loaded with grain was backing up. By now several ranch hands had gathered around the base of the silo and taken off their hats; with their mouths open they looked up at their boss, who was old enough to be their father.

"What the hell are you boys gaping at?" Bob called down from the silo.

"Well, *you*, Bob," said a hand named T. J. Eitel. "You shouldn't be up there, *should* you?"

Bob looked dismayed. "Meaning what?"

"Nothin', I guess," T. J. said, smoothing his droopy mournful mustache.

"Who should be up here, then?" Bob shouted.

"Us, I guess."

"You know I'd never let you do anything I wasn't willing to, now would I?"

"I guess not."

Later that morning, with the silo full, Bob and T. J. found the time to haul a load of live cattle up from the ranch near Colorado Springs, north of Denver, in the ranch's 18-wheeler truck. Bob drove, and T. J. sat holding the side of his face, where a sore tooth had swollen his cheek, and he suffered in silence. They had delivered about forty head in all, and facing the drive home, both men needed a break. Bob thought that a few stiff drinks would be just the thing for T. J. He had in mind a grilled buffalo tenderloin for himself. He pulled the truck to a stop by the curb in front of the elegant Palace Arms restaurant in Denver's exclusive Brown Palace Hotel. The parking valet leaped to his feet off the bench. The truck reeked of cow dung. He waved them on. Bob set the brake. He climbed down out of the cab and threw the attendant the keys.

"Park it, son," he told him.

T. J. was cupping his sore jaw. The two cowboys, dressed in filthy Wranglers, boots, work hats, and snap-button sweat-stained shirts, swept up to the maitre d', who took umbrage at their aroma.

"Yes?"

Embarrassed for himself, T. J. was thinking, Oh, God. The

old Freightliner and the way we're dressed says "cowboy" and "This is all we got."

Bob pointed out a choice table over by the windows. The maitre d' feigned studying his reservation book with an expression of doubt. He was about to put that doubt into words when he glanced up, recognizing Bob. His expression changed. "Why of course, Mr. Norris," he told him. "Right this way."

Eating hungrily, Bob did not mind the sidelong glances other diners cast in their direction. Bob enjoyed his tenderloin, while T. J. sipped on Bourbon for his sore tooth. When they were done, their napkins folded on the table, Bob paid, leaving a generous tip, and they headed south again toward Colorado Springs. By the time they arrived at the ranch both men felt that they had done a fair day's work, doing what modern cowboys were meant to do. Bob cleaned up and both men went off to bed.

The next morning Bob was late turning out. He was walking over to his office in the horse barn when a stranger drove up in a pickup. He was a compact younger man with short brown hair and the confident mien of someone who knew his way around animals. His clothes smelled faintly of an odor Bob could not identify. It had nothing to do with horses, though, or cows, for that matter. The man put out his hand and introduced himself as Barry Jackson.

"One of my men said you stopped by yesterday," said Bob politely. "What can I do for you, Mr. Jackson?"

"I'd like to rent a couple of your stalls."

Bob explained to him, "We kinda do our own thing here—cuttin' horses mostly. I don't lease stalls out." He looked at Jackson, who seemed disappointed. Bob asked him, "What kind of horses do you have?"

"I don't have horses," Jackson replied.

Bob thought, Oh, Christ. He's got ostriches. He hated ostriches and would gladly have explained why. "You just don't know what the hell they're *thinking*. Ostriches stand there and look at you, and all of a sudden they go *bing* and they've pecked your damn forehead. Or they'll kick the hell out of you. So I asked him, 'What in the hell *do* you have?' "

Jackson paused now, clearly tongue-tied.

"Well, Mr. Jackson?" Bob coaxed him.

"Six baby elephants."

Bob's eyes widened in surprise. He was momentarily speechless. To be sure he had heard him right, he asked, "Six . . . *elephants*?"

"Baby elephants, yes, sir."

"Well, now, that's *unique*."

Something unique had always been hard to find for a cowboy who was raised with a bear—a black bear, whom the Norris family named Lulu even though he was a he-bear. No one in the family even tried to find out the truth, until a veterinarian told them. Lulu took summertime naps with Bob, still a boy, under an old oak tree on a hill overlooking forty acres of deer park and pastureland of the family farm. Lulu would drape his paw over Bob's chest, and the two of them snoozed to the summer sounds of buzzing bees and the melodies of bluebirds and shrieks of jays. Lulu was a gentle, sweet bear orphan that Bob's father had adopted on the spot. Such a different decision was not out of the ordinary for the senior Norris. It was an unusual family to begin with, and the father was the most unusual of all.

Lester Norris was a farmer-artist who had drawn the cartoon characters of the *Three Little Pigs* and *Tinker Bell* for Walt Disney and then had forsaken his art for banking, business, and investment. Bob missed his dad, who journeyed to the office each morning and returned home each evening, and after an early dinner he went straight to bed. In the mornings he was gone again. To say that as a boy Bob missed his father is to miss the point. Bob did not want to grow up and do what his father did. Why have children if you could not be with them?

Though Lester Norris went back and forth to his office each day, he thought of himself as a farmer, too—a gentleman farmer. He made himself into a man of sharp contrasts—artist, cartoonist, practical thinker, farmer, and investor. His head ruled his heart, and Mammon dominated his art: Business interfered with, and then finally erased, his creative life, and from then on he would not be the same father to Bob and his brothers and sisters he would otherwise have been, and even the one he would have wanted to be. While he was at home he had little time for his large and

42

growing family and the simple way of life that the animals on the farm had come, in Bob's mind, to symbolize.

Animals like Lulu were friends of the Norris children. Lester Norris had planned for his three sons and two daughters to care for and enjoy the animals, which were at the center of their lives. Their St. Charles, Illinois, farm was home to the usual saddle horses, milk cows, rabbits, chickens, and goats, and Lulu. Bob's brothers and sisters assumed their presence and lived alongside them as their caretakers. For Bob, though, the family menagerie gave him the first glimpse of himself as a person with a profound empathy for animals.

The story goes that at an early age Bob visited the yards in St. Charles where the steam trains came in, switched, changed crews, then went out again, with the huffing of engines, the scream of iron brakes, and the clang of steel meeting coupled steel. The smell of creosote and coal, hot oil and burned wood, were intoxicating to a boy his age. There was danger there, too. Railroad employees called "yard bulls" chased down boys like Bob and beat them; the boxcars themselves carried hobos; and heavy steel wheels could never be stopped in time to save the life of a boy who happened to get in their way. Bob hung around the yard, watching and hoping for the unusual and unexpected.

In the late summers, the arriving trains often carried live ewes from the pasturelands to the markets in Chicago. Passing through, they halted in St. Charles to take on water and wood. Regularly a railroad man, his boots crunching in the gravel, walked down the length of the stopped trains, checking for baby lambs born on the trip. He separated them from their mothers and threw them off the train to die on the sun-baked roadbed.

Bob could not understand this wanton cruelty. At the risk of a beating or arrest, he followed the train man, sometimes stealthily, and snatched up the newly orphaned babies before they died. He ran away with them with a feeling of divine grace, and trundled them home in his arms.

Inevitably his mother, standing at the open icebox, asked him, "Who's been drinking all this milk?"

"Me," said Bob, who had secretly fed the lambs milk from the farmhouse kitchen.

Her eyes narrowed. She knew where the milk was going. She could see out the kitchen window baby lambs bouncing and skipping and jumping in the pasture.

Bob wondered about himself and this strange gift that he didn't know what to do with. He felt alone and very much apart. As he got older he took himself up to the top of the knoll where he went with Lulu, looking down over the pasture. Below him cows grazed and horses browsed, and sometimes the sky filled with clouds as white as wool. He wondered at these times about his own inner nature: He was different, he was certain of that now. He got along better with animals than he did with people. He *himself* preferred animals to his own kind. Animals did not lie and cheat and were sweet and simple, honest and forgiving. He understood them, their pleasures and their pain, their wants and their desires, and their wildness.

It was not that he did not fit in. Of course he was popular. That was not what sent him to the top of the hill in wonderment. He did not *want* to fit into the real world of his businessman father. The real world to Bob was animals and the land. And the question that he asked himself was, How could he make a life for himself in this animal world that was also *his* world?

Lulu was a true friend. But he was also a bear. And as he grew and got stronger and could snap his steel chain like twine, he wandered off when and where he liked, until one day he frightened the Norris's neighbors. Bob's father feared for an accident, and what would happen to Lulu then? Would the sheriff shoot him? Bob attended school in the day, and Lulu wandered alone, until one day the neighbors reported him again. The sheriff advised Bob's father to get rid of him, and reluctantly Lulu was sent to the Elgin, Illinois, zoo.

The loss of Lulu devastated Bob, who could not understand why he had to go. He and Lulu had understandings, boy to bear; emotions tied them in profound and mysterious ways. The bear loved ice cream cones and honey on a stick, and his joy seemed so pure. No, Lulu had long since ceased to be just an animal to Bob, if he ever was. Bob had sighted Lulu's wild inner nature; and it somewhat mirrored his own. That's what crushed him about Lulu leaving the farm—loved ones did not give up on the ones they loved for being who they were.

In the spring a year after Lulu went away, Bob's teacher announced a field trip to the Elgin zoo. Bob was as excited for Lulu as for himself. When the day came, and the class traveled by bus, Bob said nothing to any of his classmates about Lulu. Even when, after walking from one pen to another, they reached the bear exhibit, which was typical of outdoor pens with a small moat, a *faux* cave, and rocks to make it seem like nature in the raw. The class pressed against the iron fence. Lulu was sitting outside in the sun. He spied Bob, or caught his scent, and he growled what Bob interpreted as an invitation to join him in the cage. He was thrilled to accept, with what appeared to the other children to be an act of madness. He scrambled over the fence as Lulu shambled over to him wagging his tongue with what could have been either happiness or hunger. Bob reached out to him, called his name, and scratched behind his ears. Lulu licked his face. And the zoo attendant, who knew nothing of Bob and Lulu's history, swooned.

"Don't move, kid. I'm comin'! Don't move! Be calm."

"Okay," Bob said. He laughed and hammed with Lulu while his classmates watched in horror. He never explained, and the mystery of his magical ability to tame wild animals gained him a wide reputation, especially vibrant among the girls, as the most unusual boy for miles around.

He was a towheaded kid, full of mischief, who liked the spotlight more than school, books, and teachers. He loved the outdoors and physical action. He was wild. One of his favorite jobs was working for the Dunham Woods hunt club as the "fox," dragging a gunnysack of scented bait behind his horse. Bob thought as a fox would think, running from the jaws of the dogs, which he outwitted by crossing water and laying a circular baited trail for them to follow. He put himself in the mind of the fox, of *being* the fox. The club's master of the hounds finally told him to make it easier. The fox that was never caught was disappointing the hunters.

By now Bob was empathizing with all animals, no matter whether they were exotic or just barnyard beasts. They came to him, communicated with him through their actions as signs. They gave him their trust, even putting their lives wholly in his hands.

He started spending time with his grandfather. Robert Angell was a big man, set in his ways, who had been a real cowboy in his younger days on 3,500 acres in California's coastal Santa Lucia Range. He was retired now, and waxed philosophical with his grandson. He kept stacks of old pulp magazines about the romance of the Western cowboy, which Bob read. He told stories about his ranch, his saddles, silver bridles, and lariats, and what life was like in the old days. Some evenings they huddled in front of the Emerson radio listening to programs like *The Lone Ranger*. The radio dramas were much more than entertainments. Bob was listening to the adventures of other men and boys living lives that he wanted to lead. He wanted to be a cowboy.

Around campfires later, Bob would talk about that point at which the fantasy of the cowboy meets the reality. The virtue of self-sufficiency was at its core. "I don't want to sound corny, but," was how Bob started out. He was serious, continuing, "As a cowboy you have to rely on yourself. You get in situations just naturally that nobody's going to get you out of. You got to handle whatever comes up."

He remembers a day, long ago, when the fantasy of his life came together with reality in a moment of urgent need. He trusted his life to an animal: He was out on a mare named Mrs. Honey, checking fences in the national forest adjacent to his own land and breaking the crusts of ice on the waterholes when a blizzard blew out of the north and caught him by surprise. Within minutes he could see nothing. The wind whipped the snow into his face. Mrs. Honey bowed her head against the ice slivers, which felt sharp enough to scratch the skin.

Lost and in danger of freezing to death, Bob turned the mare loose on the reins. He told her, "Take me home, Mrs. Honey."

He pulled up his collar, clasped his jacket, and lowered

his chin to his chest. His hands were frozen in leather working gloves, and his feet felt like stones in the stirrups. His
eyebrows were thick with ice. He could have sworn Mrs.
Honey was going the wrong way. He wanted to stop her and
tell her to turn, but he did not know where to go. And so he
went with her judgment. At that moment the world contained no humans but himself, and he felt so much in tune
with his horse that he might have been one himself. He
knew she would protect him, trying to get home.

Hours went by, as the weather worsened and horse and
rider wandered. The snow blew in drifts. Mrs. Honey stag-
gered and Bob hunkered over, not even trying see their
direction anymore. He thought they were going to die.

Suddenly Mrs. Honey stopped. Bob woke out of a frozen
stupor. He thought she was finished—that they both were
as good as dead, and that she was standing now, waiting to
die. He pushed up the brim of his hat. He could hear the ice
and snow crack on his hatbrim and his collar. In front of
the mare's nose stood the gate to the corral.

The cowboy and his animals lived for one another. Their
life was simple, needing only a horizon. "It's two in the
morning, and you get up out of a warm bed and ride
through the snow and run your hand up a cow's butt to pull
a calf, and the snow's blowin' on your neck and it's twenty
below zero; the cow's trying to gore you, and the horse's
kickin', and you get run over in a corral, and kicked, and you
do it. You do it because you love the life.

49

"Not to go on about this, but a little while ago, I was on my horse, Big Bob, sortin' cows, and I was wearing my rock grinder spurs in tight quarters; I should have worn my ball spurs. This big ol' calf spun around and jammed up against me, and she caught my foot and I ran that rock grinder in Big Bob's side and he spun around like *that*, and I was off, hangin' on, and the corral is about ten feet wide with steel posts, and he spun me off, and I didn't want to get dragged, and Bob's stompin' on me while he's spinnin', and I hit that goddamned post right on the top of my head. And sumbitch, it raised a knot."

A flamboyance that Bob had inherited from his mother's family energized his fantasy of the cowboy's life. His grand-uncle John Gates, called "Bet a Million," symbolized the buccaneering spirit of the West that Bob yearned to take part in before it was too late. Gates was as brash as he was flush, a gambler to the core who bet the ranchers around San Antonio that he could stampede a herd of longhorns into a stock fence made of thirty strands of the barbed wire he wanted to sell them. They took his bet, and when the wire held against the steers, the wire made Gates a fortune, which he parlayed into railroads, steel, and oil in a company plainly enough called the Texas Company.

After his death in 1911 part of his wealth was passed on to Bob's mother, who had been his favorite niece.

And Gates's little oil company in East Texas by then had changed its name to Texaco.

———

There was no room in the Ivy League for Bob's horse, and he was not going away without his horse to Yale, which had recruited him as a swimmer. So he went instead to the University of Kentucky, where horses *were* allowed, and for four years he studied animal husbandry and agriculture. In some respects he already knew more than his teachers. The habits and behavior of horses and cows, and their thoughts and peculiarities, were as familiar to Bob as he was to himself. In class he learned the animals' anatomies, their bones and musculatures. He was trying, through the formal study of animals, he guessed, to study himself.

He wanted to be a cowboy, but he was, after all, the son of a rich businessman. Bob did not know how to become what he wanted to be, and he hoped the university might show him a way, since that was what higher education was meant to be for. Meanwhile he bided his time.

For one thing he played football at Kentucky for Paul "Bear" Bryant (Bryant coached at Kentucky before his celebrated tenure at the University of Alabama), who taught him more than just the game.

In the spring of his freshman year, while the team was practicing in a snow flurry on a field under Bryant's flinty eye, one of Bob's teammates was knocked unconscious. Bob ran to his aid. He was easing the player's helmet off when Coach Bryant, sitting on his perch, shouted at Bob, who recalled him saying, "Don't touch that man!"

"Yes, sir, I'll get a stretcher," said Bob, misunderstanding.

"No you won't. Keep playing."

Another thirty-five minutes went by until Bryant finally hollered, "Break!"

Bob ran for a stretcher. Covered with wet snow, his friend was still unconscious. Bob lifted him up, carried him off the field, and laid him down in the backseat of his car. When they reached the hospital, doctors diagnosed a concussion.

Bob could not sleep that night. He was angry, and he was torn and sad for his teammate and his coach. He loved to play football, but he had lost respect for Bryant. The next day he walked into Bryant's office carrying his football uniform and told him to "shove it." "Coach," he went on, "that man is a friend of mine. None of us mind getting hurt, but what you did was *wrong*."

In the summer of 1949, he signed on as a cowboy riding the chuck wagon on the Waggoner's 3-D Ranch in Vernon, Texas, to get a *feel* for the life. From the start it was as he had expected, and more, all the years he had waited for the fantasy to come true, all of it—the cattle drives and stampedes, sleeping in a Tucson bed (the hard ground with a saddle for a pillow), chuck wagons, and the potwalloper's gracious grub call, "Come an' git it afore I drap it in the dirt!" The ranch manager turned the wranglers out of bed with a kick, to the sound of a clanging breakfast triangle at three in the morning. Bob was "duckin' rattlesnakes" to reach his horse on the remuda and saddle up. He rode a horse named Coyote. They shifted fifteen hundred almost wild steers under bone-dry skies. Sleeping rough, again with rattlesnakes and horned toads, eating beans off metal plates, alongside men who were older and rougher than himself, Bob kept his mouth shut and his eyes open. The regular hands on the 3-D had little use for a college boy until he earned their respect through his actions as a man and a cowboy.

That moment came for Bob at the end of the summer during cattle-shipping time. The ranch manager was opening a gate to allow the herd to cross a two-lane county highway. A white sun rising on an eastern horizon meant another hot and dusty day ahead for the cowboys and the cows. Bob was riding drag on Coyote as usual, behind the herd. The steers were moving forward at their grudging pace through the gate.

Other cowboys were working that morning, but Bob was the first to look up the highway. Not a car had gone by for hours. Now he froze at the sight of a gaudy red Buick convertible speeding at one hundred miles an hour, headed straight—and, Bob thought, unavoidably—for the steers. The driver saw what he was about to hit and sounded his horn. At the sudden shocking sound, the steers exploded back into the gate in a frenzy, stamping straight toward Bob and Coyote, and a couple of his cowboy companions.

With skill and speed Bob moved Coyote out of the way, as the steers kicked up a cloud of dust. Everything had happened fast. Bob spurred Coyote, who knew what he was being asked to do. They ran along with the stampede over a mile. Bob and the two other cowboys slowed them down by turning them, and finally stopped them.

The ranch manager, whom Bob looked up to, told him, "You know how to cowboy now. Come on into the office later and I'll start to teach you the ranchin' business."

The next summer he worked for the legendary cattleman Colonel Jack Lapham on the Flying L Ranch in Bandera, Texas. Lapham was a fighter pilot in World War I and a flying instructor in World War II, and halfway through the summer, he saw promise in Bob, deciding that the time had come, of all unlikely things for a cowboy, for him to fly.

Bob had no burning desire to learn; indeed, at first he had the impression that the colonel was taking him up for a joy ride in his wood-framed and fabric-covered Piper Cub J-3. Up in the air the colonel told him to take over the controls. Bob's cowboy boots were too big to fit the rudder pedals on the floor. As the Cub waffled in the air, he hurriedly slipped off the boots and flew the plane barefoot in a wide circle, with the colonel quietly instructing him over his shoulder. And when they landed, after three hours of instructions, the colonel got out and lit a cigarette and took a couple of drags.

"Take it up," he told Bob, sitting in the airplane.

"What did you say?" Bob asked.

"The airplane. Take it up."

"You think I'm ready for it?" Bob asked, because he certainly didn't think so himself.

"Yup," said the colonel. "You just take it up, and don't go flyin' around the country, neither."

"Well, all right," said Bob. He shut the window and somehow left the ground. He didn't fly around the country. Yelling out loud with relief, he brought the Cub in to land with a bump and a shudder. He taxied up to where the colonel was standing, cigarette still in his fingers. He opened the window and smiled, and asked the colonel what he thought.

"Now you can fly," he told him.

When he had calmed his nerves, Bob had the sense that the experience of flying solo applied to being a cowboy too. You didn't talk about it or study it, you just did it.

Girls went weak in the knees at the sight of Bob and his brother, Lester, Jr., nicknamed Brud. The girls' parents, though, often went weak in the stomach at the mention of their names. The boys' reputation for recklessness preceded them: They rode horses fast and drove cars faster, and they chased girls with lightning speed. They played hard, and fought with bare fists over girls, and often won their choices. Bob knew what young women looked good to him.

Because he knew he had a fine eye for horses, he believed that he had a fine eye for women. He appreciated both on approximately the same terms, as he said, "with no disrespect meant to either one." He knew horses even better than women, and when choosing a woman, he compared her with a filly. He looked for style, class, and spirit. He said, "If a woman has class and style, she stands out. You know, *eye* appeal. That's different for every man alive. What suits me to a T may not suit you to a T. And that's why everybody doesn't want the same woman."

A young lass whose beauty turned others pale had already caught his eye in high school. Jane Wright suited every boy's dreams, but Bob was the only one with the nerve to tell her so. He walked her home from school, and he carried her books. Before they had even kissed he made up his mind to marry her. He was a realist who knew that his parents would not let him elope. He set a date in his mind, June 10, 1950—six years away. "I just hoped I'd live to be that old. I just wanted to live long enough to get married to Jane. I prayed for it—'Just let me, Lord.' "

In the meantime Jane chose to marry another man. The betrothed couple signed the deed on a new house. Invitations went out; flowers were ordered; wedding gifts piled up on the Wrights' dining room table. Jane bought a gown with a long train.

Bob was dreaming up ways to split them apart.

"I might have killed him, or he might have killed me. I

think I'd have killed him. He was a no good sumbitch. No, I *know* I would have killed him. But anyway—I got lucky."

At the last moment Jane realized that she was making a mistake. She called off the wedding, and as soon as her parents recovered from the shock, she accepted Bob's proposal without regrets in 1950. A couple of years went by, with Bob managing a farm in Illinois, before he decided that his future lay in the West as a cowboy, and he and Jane drove out to Colorado to find a place to start a ranch and begin a family.

In time they settled on a spread near Colorado Springs, which would become one of the larger cattle ranches in the whole of Colorado. Bob registered the "T Cross" brand for his cattle. The ranching life was all that he and Jane had hoped for. The wide-open spaces were a blessing to Bob, of animals galore, blue skies and vast horizons, tumbleweeds and sage, children and family. The great Texas longhorn herds had once traveled to railheads over their land, and the Western legends of Cripple Creek, Pike's Peak, and the Black Forest gave it spirit. On their own ranch, and with their own cattle and horses, they lived as people of that region had lived for a century and more.

Bob set out to raise a family, earn a reputation, and make a living as a cowboy.

He and Jane were noticed as different from the start, however. With her beauty and his handsomeness, they were as striking as any couple ever seen in that part of Colorado. His Wranglers and boots, a plain-fronted shirt with mother-of-pearl snaps, and a Resistol brand hat somehow looked better and more natural on his thin, muscular six-foot-two frame. He *was* handsome, with a broad, lazy smile, hooded brown eyes, and a complexion that the sun and wind off the Rockies had etched with ruggedness.

Jane was more muted. With the birth of their children she had matured into an elegant woman with black hair and delicate features. Anyone could see that she was besotted with Bob. She laughed at his jokes, thrilled at his daring, admired his constancy, and, always—behind the excitement and the glamor, the hard work and hard times—worried over his safety. Only part of her, the part that loved the ranch life and endured its hardships willingly, accepted the risks. A worrier with much to occupy her, as a mother of four growing, healthy children and a husband who believed in the virtue of self-sufficiency as an article of faith, Jane drew a sharp line between which risks seemed necessary and which seemed mere bravado. She and Bob never saw eye to eye on this issue, which remained with them for years to come.

She had always known what animals meant to Bob, but she was still puzzled by the time and the energy he gave them. He just sometimes seemed to lose touch with people, even with her and the children, when he was around his animals. She was almost certain he would not know what she meant if she brought it up.

She had her own work to do as a homemaker, and the

days were filled with activity. She understood his business was to raise animals on 63,000 acres of grazing land, with three thousand mother cows, and thirty to forty horses in all stages of wildness and temper. She also accepted that horses injured their riders. When Big Bob kicked Bob full in the chest and smashed his ribs and sternum, Jane nursed her husband back to health without a scolding word. But when her sons rode recklessly and fell, and came home with broken bones, she could be less understanding. Adverse to risk herself as a mother, she did not understand when those she loved took chances that she considered unnecessary.

In their community their neighbors respected the Norrises for their honesty and character. They lived as people who "wouldn't mind selling [their] pet parrot to the town gossip," to borrow a line from Will Rogers, whom Bob sounded like when he talked with the same honeyed drawl. He lived by his word, which was the bond of the Western landowner. He attended church regularly with his family, though he said that his T Cross ranch served as ample evidence of the Almighty's hand. He knew its contours as other men knew their own signatures. He watched how it was rapidly changing with the arrival of families who also wanted a piece of the West. Almost as soon as he began to ranch, Bob saw himself as a member of a vanishing breed.

A cowboy was judged above all else on the horses he kept, and the thirty or so in Bob's barn were deemed exceptional. His breed was the quarter horse, "America's horse," it was

called, the first one native to the United States, with blood-
lines that had been mixed with several European breeds.
Andalusians from Spain, Arabians from the Middle East, or
pure English or European horses held no particular allure
for Bob. He said that he was an American, and his horses
would be American as well. Generations of cowboys had
admired, and even sung, the quarter horse's virtues. Heavily
muscled for endurance, and with compact bodies and calm
dispositions of use around cattle, they ran short distances
faster than any other horse, and easily kept pace with the
short, erratic bursts of speed common to cattle. They had a
so-called cow sense, with which they anticipated the reactions of cattle.

Cows resisted separation from their own, and moved in
tight groups like schools of fish. To "cut" one from its herd
was hard, exhausting, and violent work that called for a
close coordination between horse and cowboy. Bob and his
cutting horses worked cattle with balletic grace. He commanded his mount with a slight pressure of his thighs, or
spurs, or a light touch of the reins. The horse's eyes never
moved from the cow. By feinting with its head it made the
cow commit itself to a direction; then the horse exploited
that opening to its advantage, and the job was done.

Bob trained his own T Cross horses, from "breaking"
them to the saddle to training them to perform as champi-
ons. Over the years he acquired his own methods of making
the horses do what he asked of them. He began by following
one simple rule: Never punish a horse.

He used carrots instead. "You get more out of anything alive with a carrot than with a stick," he said. He recalled how Colonel Lapham at the Flying L came out of the house each morning to greet his horses with a pocketful of carrots. "Every living thing in nature responds to kindness," Bob said.

At the start of the day out by the barn, he whistled and held a fresh carrot up for the horses in the pasture to see. They flared their ears and raced to him. He made the horses anxious to do what he wanted them to. He trained horses to the saddle by using common "horse" sense, starting in a pen.

He entered with a saddle over his arm, a hackamore, and a short rope to lead the horse. The horse was usually skittish and shy. Its eyes bulged, and it sought out the corners of the corral. Bob walked like a man with nothing to do. He talked softly, touched the horse, and at the moment when the horse relaxed, he placed a saddle on its back and ran a lead rope through the stirrups and under its belly. Then he held the horse on long reins. If the horse ran off, Bob pulled its head around until it stopped. He had control, giving voice commands and hand signals; he turned the horse to the right and to the left, and lunged it around him. This was all groundwork that paid off when it came to mounting the horse's back. Bob got up halfway in the stirrup and talked to the horse, and then swung his leg over and sat down. He repeated that four or five times. The horse understood what he was doing; there were no surprises. The horse started walking alongside another horse and rider, with the young horse's head usually forced with a rope up to the horn of the rider's saddle. If the horse reared and tried to run, it could not go far. The rope was loosened, and Bob took the reins and rode it around the corral. Now when he gave a command, the horse obliged.

"Common sense," he said.

Outside a rodeo ring, Bob did not understand the logic of the bucking bronco. He hated getting bucked off a horse: The ground was hard, and as he grew older it got harder. "That bucking that they used to do just always seemed stupid to me," he said. "It was cruel and stupid, because once a horse knows he can buck you off, you've got a problem. Teach him a good habit that you don't have to undo instead."

Bob allowed his horses to develop their own personalities and react in their own ways to the world around them.

"Every horse is built differently in its muscle and bones," he said. "So why shouldn't every horse move different?"

Big Bob, his champion quarter horse, had a character that was full of surprises. One day on Big Bob, down near a waterhole in a pasture, with two dogs along for company, Bob rode up to a steep bank. He was dozing in the sun. Suddenly Big Bob shot up the bank. With an explosion of energy he turned 180 degrees, and Bob only had time to catch the saddle horn to stay on. He knew better than to doze on Big Bob, so he didn't blame the horse at all.

Another time he was riding Big Bob, and his cowboys were pushing cattle toward him. He did not see an all-white heifer that popped over the bank "like a ghost." He was sitting lazily on Bob one moment, and the next, he says, "I was sittin' in the air ahold of my reins." He smiled at the memory. "That's Big Bob. He's grabby-assed. It comes to him naturally. His surrogate mother was goofy." And then he adds, "But his mother was a real genuine beauty."

Bob went into ranching as much to be with his children as to be with the animals. The family lived in a house that cost only thirteen thousand dollars to build. The grandeur of its setting, with the Rockies in the distance, gentle hills between, here and there covered in spring with blankets of wildflowers and in winters with sheets of whitest snow, made the house, in Bob's eyes, into a mansion. With the animals around them, Bob and his family lived together, cooked, ate, and slept, played, cried, and laughed; got sick and recovered, all within each other's sight, sound, and reach. When the children were not attending school, they were on horseback with their father and often with their mother, as Bob says, "cowboyin'."

"We worked together. We didn't have to make things up to keep us together as a family. We were fixing fences, working the cattle, doing all sorts of general ranch work, mostly around the animals; the kids helped with branding, gathering, and doctoring of the cattle. You could say I kinda grew up with my kids. Jane was a mother and homemaker. Twenty years went by, and she didn't put the same meal on the table twice. She made a career out of it. We were lucky."

From time to time, early in the mornings, the family took to the saddle and rode to a favorite wateringhole that was stocked with trout. They threw in their lines and caught breakfast, which they cooked in a skillet over a campfire. At those times Bob inspired his children with simple, home-spun truths and lessons to live by:

> *Always keep your word.*
>
> *A gentleman never insults anyone by mistake.*
>
> *Never tell a lie, then you don't have to worry about what you said.*
>
> *Don't look for trouble, but if you get into a fight, make sure you win it.*
>
> *Fun is the main thing.*
>
> *Don't complain. Complaining is what quitters do.*
>
> *If a man doesn't respect a woman enough to clean up his mouth, he doesn't respect himself.*
>
> *Be kind to children, old folks, and animals.*

The whole family took part in the spring roundup, roping the calves, branding them, injecting them to keep them healthy, then setting them back with their mothers. The work was hard, and the days were long. They ate around campfires and slept under the stars.

"The kids and me," Bob says, "we worked out our problems together, ropin' and brandin' and ridin', always around the animals. On a ranch you eat together, you work together, and play together. You're happy and sad as a unit, and it's like the modern psychologists say, 'quality time.' Hell, I knew that they'd be up and out soon enough. They'd be gone, and then it's lost. It's lost forever and for all time."

The boyhood fantasy of the mythic cowboy was never meant to be real. But for Bob it became even more real than for most other cowboys of his generation, when one bright spring day, when he was pushing quarter horses from the pasture toward the corral, he saw strangers arrive in cars near the barn. He had been expecting a visit from advertising agency men from Chicago—someone who knew Bob in Denver had recommended the use of Bob's ranch as a background for a series of still photos that the agency was shooting for Marlboro cigarettes.

Bob watched from a distance as a cowboy model took his duds out of a trunk and prepared to change. He had a bright, new neckerchief and new jeans, a shirt with ironed creases, and shined boots that were new out of a Lucchese box. Riding nearer, Bob saw that the model's complexion was strictly indoor. He carried a little suitcase for makeup that he applied with a brush.

"Howdy!" Bob greeted him from horseback.

Meanwhile, another man hurried around the corner of the barn and introduced himself as Neil McBain, from Chicago's Leo Burnett Advertising Agency, which had created the "Marlboro Man." He put out his hand as Bob dismounted. He praised the beauty of Bob's T Cross. The setting would help create the right mood. Needlessly McBain pointed to Pike's Peak to the West and the foothills of the Rockies reflecting light and shadow. The skies lit up the color of amber.

"So you figure on what?" Bob asked him.

"Shooting some photos of the cowboy here, with the barns and horses and the wildflowers in the fields, if that's okay with you."

"Be my guest," said Bob.

Following the direction of Bob's gaze, McBain said, "He's the model." He knew how painfully obvious he was to a real cowboy: The man was too handsome to be real. McBain had sought to create a cowboy out of a trunk, and clearly he had failed.

It was not the clothes, or even the handsomeness of the professional model, that bothered him. A real cowboy had a connection to the earth and to life that only a cowboy knew. When a real cowboy rode a horse, he belonged there, and a real cowboy was as one with the animals he rode and roped. No one had thought before of using a real cowboy. It just hadn't occurred to anyone in the advertising world. Models were still the standard. But the real cowboy was the figure McBain was looking for and patterning his models after.

No makeup and costuming could ever create the real cowboy's look either. For instance, the lines around Bob's eyes were byproducts of years under the sun and in the wind, staring out over vast open spaces. In truth, Bob was what McBain was looking for. He was the real thing who did not have to look the part: The part was supposed to look like him.

Bob's neighbor, fellow rancher, and friend Ordell Larsen joined Bob that morning on the corral fence, watching the advertising agency's Marlboro Man take shape. Bob remembers, "*This* was the Marlboro Man! He got rigged out from clothes in that damn trunk. I held his horse for him while he mounted. Up in the saddle he looked like a monkey on a football."

McBain told the model to dismount: Nothing looked right. He asked him to disrobe. "Your clothes are too clean," he told him. He looked over at Bob. "Hell, you're already dirty, Mr. Norris. Let's use you instead. What do you say?"

Bob grinned. "I'll try anything once," he told McBain, and he mounted up on a stout horse named Buck. The advertising pictures were taken, and when the day ended, the photographer counted hundreds of shots of Bob and Buck together, posing in fields of wildflowers.

Larsen called out when they had finished, "Norris, if you think they're gonna *use* that film of you, you're nuts."

Bob said, "You're probably right."

Months went by. Then his youngest son, Bobby, called home. "Dad, have you seen the new *Life* magazine?"

"Nope," said Bob. "I don't get it."

"Well, get it! You and Buck are on the back."

For the next twelve years, Marlboro paid Bob pretty much to be himself. In the commercials, as in his real life, he rescued stranded calves and worked the cows. He rode his own horse through fields of snow on camera and off, and through meadows of wildflowers in spring and during the

Marlboro shoots. He stopped to give his horses a drink by picturesque waterfalls and streams, snowshoed through drifts with a newborn over the saddlehorn. He threw bales of hay out of helicopter doors to snowbound cattle, under the gaze of the camera's eye. With a lariat in his hand he rode down wild horses and longhorn cows. He was the American cowpoke in the minds of a million magazine readers and TV viewers. Best of all, he was real.

His hat was his symbol, a beautiful 20X Resistol brand hat. He was never pictured without it. Then, one night at dinner in Vail, Colorado, at the Red Lion Restaurant, after the bill was paid and Bob went to the coat-check booth to retrieve his hat and coat, the hat was gone.

"Where's my hat?" he asked the coat-check woman.

"Someone took it," she replied.

Bob was holding the claim ticket.

"Some man took it," she explained. "He knew you were the Marlboro Man. He wanted your hat."

"Do you know who he was?"

She gave him a name. He was a complete stranger.

Bob discovered that the man worked in Denver, and he went to his office the next day.

A secretary was sitting behind her desk. Bob asked if her boss was in.

"Yes, but he's busy."

"No, he's not."

"You can't go in there!"

Bob opened the inner office door. The man was behind his desk. Bob's hat was hanging on a coatrack across the room. He walked in, took his hat, and put it on his head. He looked at the man and said, "Don't say anything."

It was his Marlboro hat, and as such it was important to him as the symbol of who he was. He did not like it stolen, whatever it was. The shock of recognition came when he asked himself, Am I the Marlboro Man, or am I who I am first and foremost? Obviously the hat thief had taken him for an icon, and that was not who he thought himself to be. But the question remained.

One morning that spring he opened the *Gazette Telegraph* to learn that the company his granduncle had started was in trouble. Bob knew how oilmen had joked for years that Texaco couldn't find oil at a gas station. The company owned hardly any reserves. So Texaco had sought to buy Getty Oil, which was awash in crude still in the ground. But there was one problem with the purchase/sale: Getty was already promised to another buyer, Pennzoil, which promptly sued Texaco for "tortious interference." A Texas judge levied a fine of $11 billion in damages against Texaco, which could only pay by selling itself off in little pieces, and that meant the end of Texaco forever. That judgment started the OK Corral of Chapter XIs—the biggest bankruptcy in history—and the beginning of Bob's reluctant career in high finance.

His interest in Texaco, because of his granduncle, went deeper than stock and assets. His father had sat on its board. The Texaco brand was part of the Norris family legend. Bob had no use for the company's managers, who he felt were seriously out of touch with reality. How could they have done such a stupid thing? he wanted to know. Of course they knew that Pennzoil had already tendered an offer for Getty, which had been accepted. Why take the risk?

The company's CEO did not feel beholden to the shareholders, Bob was convinced, and that angered him. These were thousands of small and large investors who stood to lose everything, and Bob felt responsible to them as individuals. He was not just one man or one investor. He was the grandnephew of Texaco's founder, and it was up to him to defend the company from itself.

Bob hated the business world. He seethed when Texaco's CEO told him he was "naive" and warned him to stay out of the fray. Of course he was naive: He was a cowboy who knew animals, not balance sheets. But he knew that he had a few lessons to teach, and he replied to Texaco's CEO with straight talk. "You put on your pants one leg at a time, same as me," he told him. "Hell, *yes*, I'm naive. I *know* I'm naive. But I also know the smell of bullshit. I call a spade a spade. I learned a long time ago not to tell a lie. You never have to worry about what the hell you said when you always tell the truth. Guys like you live in a different world. You lie, and you set people up, and you do all kinds of underhanded things.

You don't know how to deal with someone who is straight. It makes you squirrelly."

As it happened, Carl Icahn suddenly became one of Texaco's larger stockholders, quickly loading up his portfolio with Texaco stock in hope of a windfall brought about by the calamity of the bankruptcy. Icahn, the fabled greenmailer, maverick investor, and takeover king, viewed the "little stockholders" like Bob as hayseeds who were over their heads in New York City's corporate offices.

But Texaco's Equity Committee had already elected Bob its chairman, before Icahn had bought in. At one of the committee's later meetings in the Waldorf Hotel, Icahn took his place at the other end of a long table and began to harangue the whole committee. He shook his finger at them, scolding them as if they were dunces. Bob leaned over on his hip, reached in his pants pocket, and pulled out a steel-handled knife ten-inches long. Honed on a whetstone sharp as a razor and needle-pointed, the knife was designed to carve meat. As Icahn watched, Bob jabbed the knifepoint into a stack of documents on the table. "We're not going to take this from you, Carl," Bob told him. "If you try this again I promise you I'll not mess with these lawyers around this table. You and I will settle this personally."

Icahn left the meeting, but ten minutes later he called Bob to apologize, then asked, genuinely confused, "Why don't you like me?"

"Hell, I never said I didn't like you, Carl. You're just like a pet rattlesnake, that's all. But I appreciate the apology anyway."

"Why don't you go back and run your ranch? Let me run Texaco."

"I respect you and your word, Carl, but I know you'll pull Texaco apart."

"Oh, God, Bob. I'd *never* do that. I'd need to raise thirteen billion dollars to do that, and it would take months."

Bob said, "Gee, Carl, we all have our problems."

As the bankruptcy negotiations dragged on, Bob saw that Texaco's CEO did not want to settle. He wanted the U.S. Supreme Court to decide on the matter instead, while everyone else seemed to acknowledge that the Supreme Court probably would never even review the case. Clearly someone had to step in. "We're running out of time and bullets," Bob told the Equity Committee.

In a bold, straightforward move, Bob sat down with Pennzoil's CEO and founder. Face-to-face, he named a settlement figure—$3.01 billion. "Take it or leave it," Bob told Hugh Leidke.

The money would come from the portfolios of shareholders like Bob. But settling for $3 billion was better than paying the original $11 billion levy. The figures whirled in front of Bob's eyes as the two men talked. To his utter relief, after a tense moment's deliberation, Leidke said, "Bob, I can live with that."

Now the bankruptcy fight was over.

Bob was no longer Texaco's Man in the White Hat.

And something more—he was no longer the Marlboro Man.

One morning Bob woke up to facts that were only then emerging about the dangers of smoking cigarettes. These were not part of the cowboy myth that Bob believed in. What was this Marlboro thing that had been good to him for twelve years? he asked himself one day as he looked in the shaving mirror. Then during a week when he was traveling on a commercial "shoot" in Texas, he told the advertising agency's producer, "This is going to be my last deal." He thought, My kids are calling me a hypocrite to my face, and they are right. Being the Marlboro Man is a kick, but the kick is over.

The producer seemed amazed. "No one ever quit as a Marlboro cowboy before," he told Bob.

"That's probably true," Bob replied.

"You can't."

"I just did."

The Old West had changed. The young ranchers now were raising kangaroos, ostriches, and llamas; they worked the stock markets on Wall Street as well as the stockyards. People were being told to avoid red meat. Cheaper beef was coming over the borders of Mexico and Canada. The Marlboro Man was a broken icon. His children now had their own children; he was older; his horse Big Bob was sunken eyed and getting swaybacked. No one needed Bob quite as they used to.

Where had the time gone? he wondered. The kids and Jane and I were having a good time and then the end of it rolled around awfully fast, and it left a void. It was the same with life. It just came and went, it seemed, and I was too busy living it to watch it pass by.

He thought about it. The lambs rescued, Lulu lost, his horses now old and tired, and the herds of cows moved on—he was an animal lover, and it was over. "It just came and went."

He asked himself, What more can there be?

CHAPTER THREE

Amy searched with the tip of her trunk for the lost scents of her mother, the Sengwa, and the river below the falls. Her eyes could not see over the steel door. She tentatively explored the air and paused her trunk over the nose of a horse standing in front of the stall. Its smell blended with baled alfalfa and the pungence of Western cows. The horse flared its nostrils. Amy's trunk turned inquisitively upward to catch the scent of Bob's aftershave. He was sitting on Big Bob, and when he spoke to her, she lowered her trunk out of sight below the door.

Bob had attended the unloading supervised by the owner of the baby elephants. They had arrived in a horse trailer, backing down the ramp into the morning sun one by one. This new place smelled and looked not unlike Africa, with puffy cloud-filled skies and green hills, dun grass, and sagebrush. The sounds of motors, which the babies feared, and of men, of whom they were uncertain, filled the dry cool air that came off the snow-peaked mountains. The six babies searched for a place to hide.

Bob had never felt sorrier for any living creatures. These six orphans were just babies without any grown-up creature like themselves to lead them. Everything they smelled and saw must have seemed very strange. Bob felt the natural urge to calm them, but he knew he would make them more afraid if he tried. He watched as their owner pulled them along by their trunks into the barn gallery and straight down the covered walkway to the stalls.

Bob stood on the outside looking in. "They sure are cute," he said.

"They're not properly weaned yet," their owner, Barry Jackson, said. "They'll eat some hay, but they need milk." He looked around him. "I got buckets in my truck. They need to be fed right now."

Of course they would be hungry. They had come from Africa only days ago, Jackson told Bob, who could not take his eyes off them. He did not know what it was that attracted him to them. He had never seen an elephant up close like this before, and he decided that baby elephants were just more of almost everything than he had ever imagined. They looked at him with expressions that he thought showed intelligence and emotion, as if they were asking him, with their brown eyes, to protect them.

Both men got to work. The milk was poured into the

buckets, and Bob fetched oats and grain from the horses' bins and filled a tub with fresh water. By the time he got back to the stalls, Jackson was squatting down feeding one of the babies. The milk was sloshing out of the bucket onto the floor. He was impatient, cursing under his breath.

Bob patted the baby elephant's head, stroked her side, and talked to her. "It's okay, it's okay," he said, just as he would talk to a skittish colt. He looked at Jackson. "I think you might want to be a little more patient with that," he said. "She's scared and too upset to eat right now."

Jackson darted him a glance.

"Mind if I try?" asked Bob.

Jackson stood up, clearly glad to hand over the task.

Bob stayed with the baby for an hour or more. When he next looked up, Jackson was gone. The little baby had eaten some of the oats and drunk half of the milk in the bucket. She was calmer now, but when he touched her skin she trembled and shied away. He straightened up. "Quiet down, now," he told her. "I'll be back in a minute."

Jackson was getting ready to leave.

"What's their feeding schedule?" Bob asked him.

"I'll come back, if that's what you're asking."

"I was asking how often they need to be helped to eat. I'm not trying to get in your way, Mr. Jackson. They're your animals, and you're renting the stalls from me, fair and square."

Jackson sighed. "They need constant attention," he told Bob. "But it's not possible, not the way things are. They'll

77

have to get by. I'll be around a few times a day. They'll be fine."

"Then what are your plans for them?" asked Bob.

"Sell them off. I already put out the word. It shouldn't take long."

"To a zoo?"

"Or a circus. I've got my price, and anyone who meets it is fine with me."

"What is it—their price—if you don't mind my asking?"

He paused a couple of seconds. "Eighteen thousand dollars each."

Bob whistled through his teeth. He had no idea what elephants cost. Maybe eighteen thousand dollars was a bargain; he calculated more than a hundred thousand dollars in total for the six elephant babies.

"How the heck did you get here?" asked Bob. Baby elephants in southern Colorado? For an importer to bring them here all the way from Africa to sell them to zoos and circuses required a word or two of explanation.

"I'm pretty sure they'll sell in Mexico," Jackson replied. "They have a lot of circuses with animals down there. I hope so, anyhow."

"And this is the closest you could get them?" Bob persisted.

"This is where the airplane landed. I didn't want to load them up in another airplane without knowing where I'd be selling them."

Bob nodded. In the end it didn't matter. They were his

boarders now, and he felt partly responsible. "It's quite an investment you've got there," he said.

"Yes, sir."

"It's worth looking out for."

He nodded. "I didn't count on it getting this cold. Elephants don't like the cold. It's why I'm renting the covered stalls from you—to keep them warm."

Jackson said good-bye, and Bob went back into the barn.

After checking on the babies one last time that evening around dusk, he went home to tell Jane. He knew she would be excited, too. She collected elephant figurines on a marble-topped table in a corner of their living room and over the years had acquired a miniature herd of Asian and African elephants, babies and cows and bulls. Taken together as a group they represented the many sides of a long elephant-human history. There were cute, cuddly Dumbo figurines in light pastels, and some of idealized, helpless baby elephants that were hardly meant to seem real at all. Then there were proud, aggressive bulls with trunks raised and ears out as if they were frozen in the act of charging; and there were female elephants, rounder than the bulls, and yet commanding too, sheltering their young by their sides. Altogether the table tableau was a conversation piece hard for anyone visiting the house to miss.

Jane loved her elephants' mystical appeal. It was said that Asian elephants brought good fortune to pregnant human mothers who walked under their bellies three times.

By extension, they brought luck in general. But they had to be facing east, the superstition went, or else the magic was gone. If by some chance in dusting them, one of her figurines was turned away from facing the right direction, Jane always turned it back.

To Bob the figurines represented something different. The idea of elephants appealed to him as great beings that were both powerful *and* vulnerable in the sense that they were easily hunted, sighted, and shot, yet they were strong enough to defeat any enemy on even terms.

"They're hardly bigger than the figurines," he told Jane, wanting her to understand that the orphans were not difficult to manage. "Wait till you see them," he said. "They're *so* darned cute. They come up to my belt buckle."

Jane almost laughed. She could see he was already falling in love. But she focused on the practicalities of keeping the babies: It was October and getting cold at night, and the babies did not have mothers to take care of them. "How will they survive?" she asked Bob.

"I'll put heat lamps in their stalls to keep them warm."

"What about their owner?"

Bob told her, "To him they could be any damn thing."

"What a shame."

Jane saw in Bob's eyes at that moment an excitement that had gone out of them in the last months. The arrival of the baby elephants had revived his curiosity; he had found new animal friends like old Lulu.

"The grandchildren would love to see a baby elephant," she said.

"Better not say anything to them yet," Bob told her. "I don't know how long they'll be here."

Barry Jackson had agreed to pay Bob five hundred dollars a month to rent the horse stalls while he waited for buyers to show up. There was no telling how long that would take. African elephants were much less sought after than Asians. According to the conventional wisdom, Africans were intractable beasts both as performers and as zoo curiosities, while Asians, rare and endangered, were the pachyderms of choice in captivity. If these assumptions held, the baby elephants could be boarders at the ranch for some time to come. And while that worried Jackson, it suited Bob fine, because, more than being merely curious, he was drawn to the orphans.

From a perch on the fence around the little elephants' enclosure, he found himself getting to know them as distinct individuals. He could see their intelligence. Each one had a different personality and character. One of them was a clown. She hooked her hind legs on the bottom rail of the fence and swung her trunk, playing with it. Another baby was quiet and serious, and one of them was skittish and shy.

As he observed them in the paddock, he began to focus his attention on one of them in particular. She was different from the other five. She was the runt, smaller and less assertive. The other five babies pushed her away. It was clear to Bob that this one in particular was going to have the hardest time adjusting to a new life.

He told Jane, "She's the littlest. She's kind of . . . well, *beautiful*. She has long eyelashes. Real pretty amber eyes. Good lookin'. She is a real little lady. She has charm. The others kind of knock her around."

The next day he watched her alone in the stall and attended her feedings, standing on the other side of the door while Jackson dipped her trunk in the milk buckets. Bob encouraged her to eat oats from his palm. She was not gaining weight as she should, Jackson told him. Something was wrong. She would not leave her stall unless she was forced out into the paddock with the other elephants. Bob bent over the door and talked to her. Jackson said that the stall must have reminded her of the crate in which she had traveled from Africa. She was afraid of open spaces.

Bob knew the seductive power of a carrot with horses. He sliced a carrot with his knife and gave the baby elephant a piece. She ate it tentatively, then she held out her trunk for more.

"Now I've got you," he told her. He stepped into the stall. She reached out her trunk for the carrot. Bit by bit, step by step, he got her to leave the stall on her own. He kept the door open. She could go back in anytime. He watched her out in the paddock. She was curious. She looked up at the sky and lifted her trunk to smell the air. But at the sight of a ranch hand riding past on his horse, she folded her ears, lowered her head, and ran back into her stall.

In the days that followed, with the baby now entering the paddock on her own even without the inducement of carrots, Bob left off training his cutting horses to watch her from the corral fence. Some of his ranch hands joined him on the rails. There were the usual jokes and laughter, which this time Bob found annoying.

"Cut it out," he ordered his hands. "She may be a curiosity, but she's no joke. She's a beautiful animal. Use your eyes."

He was watching the baby with a horse trainer's eye to see exactly what made her different and appealing. Earlier the colts in the round pen had panicked at the sight of her. With shrieks of sheer equine terror, the young horses had leaped like kangaroos over a six-foot pipe fence to get away from the sight of her. The little runt stood aloof, while the other babies had huddled together for safety. The colts frightened her, Bob could tell, and he tried to understand her fear. He knew how he would feel if his own kind avoided him. Built into the runt's character, he believed, was an awareness of herself as different.

Bob worried about who would protect her. She had no adult elephant to come between her and the other babies, who behaved as they would never have been allowed to in the wild. They ganged up on her, took her food, and hit her with their trunks. They behaved as orphaned elephants did in the wild.

For want of an adult elephant as her protector, Bob made certain that she got her fair share. He shouted at the other babies to move aside. His presence in the paddock on a horse forced them to back away. Using his skills as a cowboy, he cut the other elephants away to allow her time to eat and drink. He visited her stall, where she was separated for her own protection. He visited her in the late afternoons and evenings when the sun was setting. He fed her carrots. He talked to her. She moved closer to him and lifted her trunk to smell him.

Until now he had not stopped to wonder if she had a name. He asked Jackson when he next came by.

"Amy," he replied automatically.

"Nice," said Bob, then tried out the name aloud a couple of times. "It fits her, don't you think?"

"If you say so, Mr. Norris."

"Where does it come from? Amy?"

"I don't know. Someplace. It was written on her crate."

As a rancher and horseman, Bob believed that "no better word was ever spoken of a man than that he was careful of his horses." He added goats to that list, and dogs, cats, and cows, "any damn thing except rattlers and ostriches," he liked to say. Now he included one baby elephant on this list as well.

On a day when the sun was warmer than usual and the sky was bright he paused a moment to watch as Jackson chased Amy around in her paddock. She was terrified, Bob guessed, because men on foot running like Jackson had killed her family. She was trying to get away to a corner of the paddock.

Amy did not belong to Bob; she was a strange animal, and he did not know her behavior, but he knew a frightened, traumatized baby when he saw one. He climbed the fence rail and poised himself to jump down into the paddock. He watched as Jackson, chasing her, raised a length of two-by-four. Bob straightened up. Jackson swung and hit Amy hard across the rump.

Bob was off the fence and running across the paddock. He snatched the board out of Jackson's hands. He was trembling with anger and had trouble controlling his voice when he told him, "You hit her again, Mr. Jackson, and we're going to have a problem." He threw the board over the fence and walked off in disgust. Jackson stood there looking between Amy and Bob. He did not know what was happening, but he sensed the presence of powerful emotions that he did not grasp. These elephants were a commodity to him, and he could not comprehend anyone feeling protective of them simply as animals. He got in his truck and drove off. He would not hit her again.

Amy was still not eating as Bob imagined she should. She was not properly weaned, and she was frightened much of the time. An occasional lassitude indicated a serious depression. She had started to come into her own, induced by the carrots, but then she had slipped back, and then further back.

He tried to understand her. He had no knowledge of where she had come from. But he imagined a jungle with vines to swing on, odd beasts, and people wearing jodhpurs and pith helmets, and natives with bones in their hair. He knew that his view of Africa was outdated, if it had ever been real. Still, Amy missed her home. She missed her family, her mother and sisters. Bob could not replace what had been taken from her, but he could act as a surrogate for them—he could be Amy's mother—for a while.

Jackson had told him about the cull in Africa. Bob would have preferred to be spared the gory details. He hated the words "slaughter" and "killing," and preferred "harvest" and "cull," which made what happened sound less cruel and wanton. Jackson told Bob about how Buck deVries had saved Amy. He described her journey through Europe to the United States with the five other babies he had bought in southern Africa.

Bob told Jane, "No creature Amy's age should have to live with such dark, horrible memories, and nothing happy to replace them with."

Amy had lost her universe. Bob imagined, as he said, that her simple elephant soul ached. She had been pushed around, transported in trucks that reeked of diesel fumes, limited to a *kraal*, packed in a tight wooden crate, and fed through her trunk as though it were a filling-station nozzle. How much more could any creature take? She had been trying to gain control of her own basic baby needs when she was captured. She was listless now, and Bob took this to mean sadness. Nightmares startled her awake. She pounded the walls with her trunk. She wanted to escape as if from memory itself.

She had not made a sound, and even knowing as little about elephants as he did, that struck Bob as odd. He checked a book on elephants out of the library. He read that they expressed themselves with a repertoire of screams, squeaks, bellows, trumpets, rumbles, and sounds below the level of human hearing. He read, "All healthy baby elephants scream; if one does not it is either sick, neurotic, or mad, and will either die or be extremely troublesome."

"She's just a little baby, a puppy," he told Jane. "She's getting sickly. I don't know what to do, but something has to be done or she'll die."

Jane listened, wanting to help but not knowing what to do.

"I mean there's no way to sweet-coat what happened to her," he went on. "In a perfect world she would have stayed her whole life with her mama in the jungle. But that didn't happen."

"What can we do?" she asked him. "She doesn't belong to us."

Bob had never been more serious in his life. "I can't undo what made her an orphan. But I can do the next best thing."

The next best thing was himself.

He owned more than enough land for a baby elephant to

roam on. He could give her the time to grow and get healthy, and once she was better—once she was over her trauma—Bob could decide what to do with her then. He talked to Jane about it. "I just think I should take advantage of a situation that's come my way," he told her. "Why Jackson drove into my ranch instead of somewhere else, I'll never know. I want little Amy to be a part of our family—I just *want* her. I know she will be a challenge. But I like challenges, and just now maybe I need one too. It's me or no one."

His appeal melted Jane, who soon was in her kitchen elbow-deep in a concoction of milk and cornmeal. She and Bob dipped Amy's trunk in the bucket, and when it was full of warm milk, they guided it into her mouth. Amy knew how to feed this way; she needed a *reason* to eat, not a technique to help her do it.

Jane told Bob, "I can almost hear her asking, *Where's my mom*? She's at the age when her mother is her whole world. It's so very sad; I think we might lose her."

The young animal was wasting away from grief, as Bob saw it. He recalled a story not long before of a llama pair that escaped from a zoo in Boston. The police had shot the male dead in the street, and the female, untouched, laid her head on her mate's neck and, with a sigh, simply died, without any reason except grief.

Bob telephoned the veterinarian who ministered to his horses and cows. "You have to be the doctor of an elephant now," he told Laura H. Harris, a blond-haired woman with pretty sky blue eyes and a cowgirl's trim figure.

She thought, An elephant in terms of doctoring isn't different from a horse. The only difference is our ability to read their reactions. We know a horse's. I know a bear's and a leopard's, because I've doctored them. An elephant's? That's another thing.

She drove out to Bob's ranch right away and looked Amy over from trunk to toes.

"Nothing's wrong with her that I can tell, Bob," she reported.

Amy was physically sound, though underweight and weak, as Bob had said. Her lethargy and depression remained in spite of her eating a little bit now and then. Dr. Harris decided against seeking out expert advice at the local zoo or, farther afield, at the St. Louis Zoo. What ailed Amy was obvious, at least to her. She needed someone in her new world as unique to her as she was unique to them.

"It's up to you, Bob," Dr. Harris told him. "If anyone can save an animal like Amy, it's you."

Bob thought, Sadness, separation, and loss have happened to animals all through history. Nature is always cruel. As humans we do the best we can. Humans caused this in her, and humans can cure this. I can feed her and make sure she is clean and watered. I can stroke her and pet her. I can lay my hands on her and give her tender loving care. But the rest is up to her.

That evening Bob talked with Jane over a quiet dinner. He told her that trying to save a baby elephant from death was one of those things that you just did without thinking about it. The future would take care of itself. He told Jane, "What I'm asking, Can we adopt her?"

Jane's first thought was, Here we go again! What could she say? She loved Bob too much to say no. "You've thought about where this will lead?" she asked.

Bob told her, "Nope, I haven't. You never know that. But if you don't open the door and walk through it, life will be pretty dull."

She smiled. "Then open the door."

No zoo or circus had offered to buy Amy. By then Barry Jackson had sold the other five elephants one by one to zoos in Mexico and a circus in the Dominican Republic. Amy stood in the paddock alone now, with nowhere to go and no friend but Bob.

Jackson was clever enough to notice Bob's attraction, and how he talked to Amy, sang to her, fed her, and, reaching through the fence rails, petted her. He hardly left her paddock anymore to attend to his chores. The horses were forgotten; the cows were left to the ranch hands. Amy had clearly become the center of his world. Jackson did not bother to mention to Bob that no one wanted to buy Amy. (What kind of an elephant trader would that kind of remark have made him?) He said to Bob only that she was sure to find a home—some inquiries had been made. It was only a matter of time. But Jackson kept to himself the simple fact—he knew—that Amy would never find a home.

One Saturday, Bob was standing by Amy's stall in the gallery of the barn when Jackson came up and told him, "I think I found a buyer for Amy."

"Oh?"

"A woman from Arizona said she's coming around to pick her up this Thursday."

Bob nodded without a word.

"She wants her for a pet."

"Really?"

"She has a little lot down in Phoenix. She keeps exotics— tigers and lions and snakes."

Bob turned to Jackson: He could not let this happen. "Let me ask you, what if I was to buy her from you instead?"

"You?"

"Yes, me. She could make her home here. She likes the place. She's used to it."

"What would I tell the woman from Phoenix?"

"Tell her, 'Don't bother to come up here.' "

Jackson thought about that for a minute, perhaps pretending to decide. "Okay," he said. "She's all yours if you want to pay what I'm asking."

A handshake sealed the deal. Then Jackson folded Bob's check, slipped it into his wallet, and boarded his truck. With a wave he headed down the road. Watching him go, Bob thought back to when he was a college kid and took flying lessons from the colonel. Just like that day in the airplane, he was now "flying solo" with a baby African elephant. The dust from Jackson's truck settled on the road. Bob scratched his head and thought, Come to think of it, Jackson never did tell me the name of that gal who was going to buy Amy. He smiled with the pleasure of owning Amy. He thought, he had stood up to Carl Icahn and the officers of Texaco and Pennzoil. He had sold quarter horses and cows at a profit. He considered himself a sharp trader. But never before had he wanted anything as much as he wanted Amy. "I got out-horse-traded," he told Jane that evening. "It's fine by me."

CHAPTER FOUR

Two cowdogs on the ranch were the first to play with Amy, and their first acquaintance was clearly not by any design of Butch, a shorthaired blue heeler with a red coat. Butch was the ranch's so-called walk-on lover. He was a hard-headed dog, Bob said, that had appeared one day at the ranch, and stayed. He minded only Bob, who had taught him to work the livestock. Jo, a Doberman, kept her distance from the hands and the herds. A sullen dog that bit when she was frightened, Jo once sank her teeth into Bob's neighbor, Ordell Larsen. "She got him right in the ass," said Bob with a laugh. "He knew he'd been nipped."

The dogs roughhoused near where Amy could watch them. They chased a green rubber beach ball that was too large for them to pick up in their mouths. They drooled on it, rolled it with their noses, fell over it, and kicked it with their legs, as thrilled as they were mystified by its movement.

Amy came out from her stall into the paddock and watched the dogs from a corner. Over days, she had learned not to be afraid of her visitors. They hardly paid attention to her and no longer barked at her. She was like a young horse, and they instinctively knew to leave her alone.

But a ball was a tempting toy for most animals. It moved without a sound. It was smooth and soft and waited for a foot or a trunk to animate it. Amy stayed by herself, always watching. Then one day a gila monster bit Jo's lower jaw, and the skin on her lip fell away. In pain and sick, she went to her bed in the barn, leaving Butch alone with no play-mate.

Amy walked up to the ball and touched it with her toe. She watched it roll across the paddock. She went over to it and hit it with her trunk. The ball rolled against the stall door. She kicked it, and it rolled over to Butch. He tripped over it, and rolled it to Amy. She kicked it across the paddock; she chased it.

Butch soon forgot the ball and chased Amy's trunk. She spun in circles, keeping it just out of his reach. He chased her immune to the boredom of repetition. He was able to fetch the ball twenty or thirty times in a row with the same enthusiasm each time. Amy's trunk was just as fun.

Soon Amy gave every indication that she looked forward to Butch's visits. She stood over the ball waiting for him.

But Butch was an unreliable playmate. Now and then, he wandered off the ranch in search of girlfriends and was absent for days. Amy waited near the ball. Bob, watching her, thought it was a hopeful sign.

Bob visited her stall from the gallery side. The sound of his voice, he thought, soothed her. He had sung to his cows on drives to settle them down when the night sky crackled with lightning, songs composed long ago to the cadence of a walking cow, songs like "The Night-Herding Song":

> *Oh, slow up, dogies, quit moving around*
> *You have wandered and trampled all over the ground.*
> *Oh, graze along, dogies and feed kinda slow.*
> *And don't forever be on the go.*

And to Amy he crooned:

> *"Once in love with Amy, always in love with Amy."*

He explained as he would to a new visitor about the seasons on a Colorado cattle ranch. Sometimes, he talked to her about what was on his mind—about state politics or the movie he had seen on TV the night before. Bob believed that Amy's eyes brightened at the sound of his voice. She stood by the door and waved her trunk in the air, he was convinced, as if she wanted to reach out and touch him.

One day, out in a converted stall at the end of the horse barn, Bob was working on his tack when he heard a sound that he could have sworn was a car horn, though he had not seen a car come up the road or heard the sound of an engine. He was cleaning up saddles, halters, ropes, and chaps that hung on pegs all neat and tidy, smelling of saddle soap, polish and neat's-foot oil. Earlier he had fed Amy and talked to her. Now, he assumed that she was playing ball with Butch.

Bob cocked his ear and pushed back his hat. He went out into the sunlight and leaned against the fence.

Amy was chasing Butch around the paddock. She let out a blast of sound that cleared up Bob's confusion. The trumpet seemed to startle Amy most of all. She stopped and looked around, as if to say, "Who was that?"

The sound of her trumpeting made him laugh. She would survive, he guessed, and might even thrive from now on.

Bob and Jane began to see other changes in her. She was eating again, and the milk buckets were replaced now by bales of hay and oats. Bob noticed that the wrinkles in her skin were smoothing out.

T. J. Eitel, the ranch hand with the sore tooth and the flamboyant mustache, helped Bob take care of her. T. J. was an expert at breaking horses to the saddle. He was tall, thin, and soft-spoken. When he reached to unlatch Amy's stall door, Bob held up his hand to stop him.

"She's wild," he told T. J. "Jackson told me that a baby elephant could kill a man with a swipe of its trunk." He nodded at T. J. "Don't think just because she's cute that she's cuddly."

"She's wild?"

"Yes."

"Then how do we tame a wild elephant?" asked T. J.

"I don't know," said Bob. "How would you think?"

"You can't break 'em to the saddle, like a horse. They aren't naturally tame like cows or dogs and cats. Hell, I don't know."

"We better think about it, then," said Bob. "I don't want her to hurt anybody without meaning to."

Jane wanted a more constant friend for Amy than Butch. He was wandering more now, and Amy was bored without him to play with. Jane asked Bob, "Can't we find her something better? Butch is either all *on* or all *off*."

Bob knew what she was referring to. Some animals, like thoroughbred horses, had their own "pets." Amy needed a companion to be with her night and day. Bob had proof of what Jane was suggesting, or he thought so, anyway. Amy had scooped grain in a little pile in a corner of her stall. Seeing it there and not mistaking it for an accidental spill, Bob had wondered why. It seemed an odd behavior, though he knew next to nothing about how elephants behaved. A few weeks went by, and he forgot all about it, until one day when he was entering her stall to clean it. A small barn mouse scurried along the baseboard. Bob stood perfectly still, watching. The mouse stopped and smelled the air, and cleaned its nose with its front feet. It dropped down and nibbled at the grain. Had Amy left the food for the mouse? Had she chosen this mouse for her companion? Maybe he was only imagining it. But about the same time he first noticed the saved food, Amy had stopped crying at night.

Still, she deserved a better friend than Butch and a bigger one than a barn mouse.

Michelle was a mellow goat with a light brown coat, a white rectangular patch on her side, white dots on her forehead and chest, and floppy ears that hung down like two spare cheeks. Bob bought her from a neighbor, and when she arrived at the ranch, she walked over to Amy and said hello with her nose. Amy wrapped her trunk around Michelle's middle, and from the first moment they met, they walked along together around the paddock like girlfriends out shopping at the mall. Michelle became Amy's "teddy bear" and her "blankie." She cuddled Michelle, and Michelle did not seem to mind, or even to notice that her stallmate was an elephant.

"Goats don't think much," Bob told Jane. "I guess that explains it. Michelle probably doesn't think that Amy is an elephant. Amy *knows* she isn't a goat. It's a nice sight to see how Amy responds to her, though, like a long-lost friend or like the family she left behind over in Africa. But she knows it isn't true. Michelle, on the other hand, doesn't know what she is, and that's why I chose her. Taking nothing away from Amy, Michelle would probably be happy with a damned kangaroo for a friend."

From that day on Amy and Michelle played together and stood by and watched over each other. One followed the other as though they were attached by a string. Sometimes, in search of scraps of food, Michelle roamed the ranch, but at night she stayed at Amy's side. It was not so much what they did together, Bob thought. They were together as constant friends.

Sometimes Michelle took her "friendship" a step too far, however, and at those times Amy corrected her. She had saved food for the mouse, but the mouse's appetite was nothing compared to a goat's. Michelle ate cans and chewed on rubber mats and assorted junk from the scrap bin. Bob always set out a big bucket of hay and oats for Amy, from which she ate through the day, whenever she was hungry. The constant presence of food was a temptation that Michelle could not resist. She viewed all food as *her* food, without noticing that Amy did not seem to like sharing.

With Amy standing at the far end of the paddock, Michelle wandered toward the barn and the bucket of food and started to eat, looking up from time to time to see where Amy was standing. Amy took notice and walked across the paddock to the stall. She nudged Michelle away from the bucket and, with her trunk firmly around her waist, she led her out the stall door and into the paddock.

"Michelle knew she was being asked to leave, and she scooted," said Bob, who watched with fascination.

Amy then returned to her stall. She shut the bottom door with her trunk to keep Michelle out, and ate her dinner in peace.

An obstinate billygoat named Larry had arrived at the ranch with Michelle, as part of a two-goat deal that Bob had made. Larry had yellow slit eyes and curly horns. He must have thought that Amy was a punching bag. Right from the start he slammed her sides and shoulders, and butted her incessantly. Amy ran from him, but Larry was fast afoot, and his need to butt superseded any other goat activity. He lived to butt. He stood up on his hind legs and, with the full weight of his body, slammed his horns into Amy. He could not help himself.

"Larry was a rat," said Bob.

A week after Larry arrived, Bob saw him butt Amy. Unlike the other times, though, now she reacted, and her attack nearly took Bob's breath away. As quickly as he had ever seen an animal move, she hit Larry with her trunk. He left the ground.

Bob thought, Good for you, Amy! You sure are learning how to take care of business!

A few days later Bob was walking by Amy's stall when he

heard the grunts of a goat in agony. He looked in and saw that Amy had pinned Larry up against the wall and was pushing him with her head.

"Ol' Larry was going, 'Unnh, unnh, unnh.' He knew he was about to die. I thought, Oh, nuts! I did not want Amy learning bad habits. I said, 'No, no, Amy,' and she backed off. Larry ran out. I never let him *near* her again. To be honest, after that he was a goner, anyway, as far as the ranch was concerned. He was bad news."

Tentatively at first, Amy began to explore her new world. She twisted bolts and unscrewed screws, turned handles and unfastened latches. She might have dismantled her stall, leaving it in a state of collapse, if Bob had not tightened down every nut and bolt with a wrench. She wandered, sniffed, and touched out of an enormous natural curiosity, seemingly missing nothing. She explored with her trunk up in the ceiling of her stall. She worked the latches on the doors, broke off doorknobs, and pulled levers. She tested water taps. She "tasted" soaps and cleaners in the tack room, and she "played" with the saddles and bridles. She pulled the windshield wipers off the trucks and tractors and reached into the open windows and turned the steering wheels.

Her favorite distraction by far, though, was a garden hose, which she had learned to turn on at the tap. She held the nozzle and squirted herself all over, and sprayed Michelle and anyone who happened to come within reach. Bob ran through the spray and turned off the water, and Amy stood patiently holding the end of the hose, clearly waiting for him to leave.

Bob gave his young elephant the freedom to roam the whole ranch. It was time for her world to expand, he believed. He didn't mind where she went. (There was nowhere to go, anyway, but into the wide open spaces.) He kept the gate to her paddock unlocked. He had no control over her. He predicted correctly that she would always return eventually to her feeding bucket.

She looked bizarrely out of place even to the cowhands who saw her every day. Some of the newer ranch hands rubbed their eyes in disbelief, seeing her for the first time. After a few days, her presence made the hands feel different and, even a bit special. She was *their* elephant too.

Amy was content. Water was abundant, the sky was filled with clouds, and her food bin was always full. She was wild and free. Bob did not discipline her. Indeed, he asked nothing of her but that she find her way in her new world. He allowed her the freedom to grow up and gain confidence at her own pace.

One morning Amy and Michelle wandered over from the paddock to the cutting pen, where Bob was working the colts. Suddenly Amy's trunk went up, and she trumpeted loudly. Bob looked over at her, surprised. He thought, Oh, damn, here she comes!

She charged the colts in the pen as though they were the zebras back in Zimbabwe. The colts "just went bonkers when they saw her coming. I mean, one jumped plumb over the fence, it wanted out of there so bad. I didn't know what Amy was going to do. Hell, I didn't know what the horses would do either. Amy knew that she was scaring them, I swear. She was having a ball. She figured that out real quick. It was as if she was thinking, Hey, these guys are scared to death of me. I'm going to have some fun with it. She ran after them deliberately and trumpeted to frighten them."

Soon after, realizing that Amy was going to have to get along with the colts sooner or later, Bob put colts in the paddock next to her. When the colts ran around the enclosure, Amy ran around in her paddock trumpeting loudly. "She got so excited she did figure eights," said Bob, who next tied the colts to Amy's paddock fence.

At first the young horses bunched up at the sight of Amy. She walked over to them and reached her trunk through the fence. She touched their noses. She tugged at their ropes. Days later she entered their paddock and rubbed up against them. Now they didn't seem to mind. They treated her with all the indifference they would have shown just another colt.

Bob told Jane, "I guess she's starting to think of herself as a horse with a trunk. Or maybe the colts are starting to think that they are elephants without a trunk. It's hard to know. It is becoming a peaceful kingdom out there, anyway, with the lions laying down with the lambs."

Jane told him, "It seems like the only one she isn't used to, Bob, is *you*."

He knew that. He had asked himself how he might best approach her. He did not want to frighten her. A misstep or a premature action, he knew, might take away her self-confidence. He had no answers. But Jane was right. It *was* time to make Amy as much a part of the human ranch as she was of the animal.

The more he considered the problem, he came to see that an old football injury might hold the key. A couple of years before, a surgeon had removed bone chips from his knee, which sometimes locked up, "just snapped shut," and forced him to walk on crutches or ride on horseback when he would normally walk. He asked himself, Why not approach Amy on horseback? Would that fool a smart young elephant like her? He decided to give it a try.

Astride Big Bob, he rode up to Amy in her paddock. He steadied the horse and leaned over in the saddle. He took Amy's trunk in his hand and soothed her with the sound of his voice. So slowly that he hardly appeared to be moving, he swung his leg over the stallion's back and lowered one leg to the ground. He was watching Amy, ready at an instant's notice to climb back on the horse. He kept his hand out to her. He came down out of the saddle with his other foot. Now he was standing slightly apart from Big Bob. He walked across the paddock with his back turned to Amy. He pushed his hat up on his head. Deciding, Now or never, he stopped, figuring that she would either run away or charge him. He made a quarter turn to face her.

She nearly bumped into him.

THE COWBOY AND HIS ELEPHANT

Bob laughed out loud. She accepted him on his own two feet. Now they could start to be best friends.

Mud gave Bob the idea. Amy had rolled in it after rain showers and where the water from the hose pooled in the dirt. He believed that she would roll in a teacup of mud if she fit. One day he decided to build a proper, African-type wallow big enough for them to enjoy together.

He flooded a natural depression in the land, about fifty feet around and three feet deep, behind the horse barn. He brought Amy out and stood with her at the water's edge. At first she splashed with her trunk and stood on the bank. Then suddenly she charged across the pond, trumpeting. She blew water at Butch, and splashed Michelle. She sprayed Bob, then lay down and rolled over in the wallow.

T. J. and the hands came to watch. They took off their boots, rolled up their pants, and waded in, up to their calves. They splashed, fell over backward in the water, and flopped around in the mud. They threw water at Amy, and she blew water at them. Then Bob was in, up to his knees, laughing. He said to his hands, "Hell, boys, you're just like a bunch of kids."

The Toys "Я" Us sales assistants thought Bob was a doting grandfather. Money seemed to mean nothing to him. He liked *big* toys—oversize harmonicas and inflatable swimming pools, plastic baseball bats, and huge rubber balls.

The staff recommended other items—educational toys, board games, and the latest promotional tie-ins from popular kids' movies. But all the cowboy wanted were *big* toys.

"Why is that?" one of them finally thought to ask him.

"For my elephant," he replied without thinking, as he tested the strength of a plastic pool for Amy's paddock.

"Yes, sir," the attendant had replied.

No one in the store really believed him. The only elephant in the area, almost everyone knew, was the one at the Colorado Springs Zoo. So they humored him and started to recommend toys that an elephant might even enjoy, rolling their eyes at each suggestion.

Over time Amy's paddock filled up with toys, like a spoiled child's playground. At Christmas, after opening their presents around the tree at home, Bob and Jane wandered down to Amy's stall with presents in their arms. They had wrapped her gifts individually and tied them with colored ribbons. Bob laid them down on the straw in her stall. The gifts excited her interest; she tugged at the ribbons with the fingers of her trunk while Bob hummed Christmas carols to set the mood.

On Halloween Bob turned the tables on her. He dressed up in a bluish gray and *very* baggy elephant suit, with an elephant's trunk that drooped down off his face, and elephant's ears that flopped to his shoulders. Amy sniffed at him and then followed Michelle into the paddock. Bob could hardly remember a time when Halloween had been this much fun.

———

She was his little girl—"little" even as her growth was beginning to worry about everyone else on the ranch. Jane was the first to raise the issue. It wasn't that Amy was big and powerful, it was that *Bob had no control over her.*

She would not leave the barn area, even when Bob encouraged her to accompany him when he rode. She went back into her stall when she was hungry, not when Bob wanted her to. Behind Bob's back the ranch hands started to call her "the Bulldozer." And, like Jane, they worried about her wildness, her size, and Bob's lack of control.

Another issue that upset Jane was that Bob was spending all his spare time with Amy. Jane was used to him working long hours at the ranch with the cows and the horses. But he wasn't giving his time to them anymore: It was all going to Amy alone.

"You know how, when a girl is married to a golfer," she asked Bob one night, "they're called 'golf widows'? I'm becoming an 'elephant widow.' It's time for you to try to figure out where you're going with Amy."

"I'm not sure what you mean."

"Amy has to be included in *all* our lives," she told him. "For a start she has to learn to live among us, and that means she has to learn discipline. One reason you spend so much time with her is that you feel responsible for her. You have to spend the time because you have no control over her. You have to watch her or otherwise there's no telling what might happen."

"That's true," he said.

"She does what she wants. But she has to learn to do what *we* want. She can't stay a wild animal forever because she isn't living in the wild anymore. She may hurt someone. You have to be able to tell her what you want and don't want from her."

"I still don't see what you mean."

"She's big and wild, *that's* what I mean! She's going to get a whole lot bigger."

"She's vulnerable, that's all, like King Kong."

"If you don't give her proper formal training, Bob, she will *be* King Kong."

Bob talked with Laura Harris, the veterinarian, on one of her regular visits to the ranch.

"What do *you* think I should do?" he asked her.

She thought it over. "You and I, Bob, grew up around horses," she told him. "We didn't grow up around elephants."

"So?"

"Well, we don't think about whether a horse will step on us or knock us over. The horse is an animal that is brought up with people and is used to them. But an elephant, you don't know its mind. Amy is wild, and she is getting real big. Jane is right. You never know what she'll do."

Bob looked pained. "I want her to be a good elephant,

not an outlaw of an elephant, or whatever it's called. I have a responsibility to give her a good life.".

Harris repeated Jane's advice. "Without discipline she's going to hurt somebody. And that's not fair to her. If she kills someone, you're going to have to shoot her. That's how it goes."

On one of her visits to the ranch, Bob's elder daughter, Carole, saw what her father didn't want to see. Her mother told her about Amy and asked what she would do. Carole had no advice to give. Besides, she had other concerns. She was trying to find a gift for Bob's upcoming sixty-fifth birthday. He was hard to buy for: He had everything he wanted. Did Jane have any ideas?

Her mother blurted out, "Find somebody to help him with Amy."

As the birthday approached and Carole still had not found a gift, one night, watching a TV documentary entitled *Elephant*, she sat up and listened closely.

A research biologist was explaining about elephants in captivity. "Elephants are dangerous. They are big. Many people are killed every year by them. It is not something well known. They seem like cartoon characters, like Dumbo, very gentle. If they are trained properly, they are." The documentary's narrator went on, "To teach their zookeepers how to train elephants safely, the Point Defiance Zoo in Tacoma, Washington, hired trainer Richard L. Maguire."

Maguire was then shown on TV "working" the zoo's wild

bull elephant as if it were a trained dog. As the camera captured him on film, Maguire called to the bull, and he came. He ordered him to "stretch out," and he lay down. Carole thought, He can make this wild elephant do anything he wants! Richard Maguire told the camera, "This is essentially a wild animal. They can be taught, and for everyone's safety, they *should* be taught."

Carole said to herself, I just found Dad's birthday present.

She reached for the telephone and called the local PBS station. And after more than a dozen calls, she got Maguire himself on the other end of the line.

"I want to hire you to help my father train his elephant," she told him.

"You're kidding," said Maguire. "No private person *owns* an elephant."

"My dad does. Her name's Amy."

"Most of what I deal with are zoos and circuses."

"Will you do it?"

"I don't know."

"Please?"

"Let's just say I'm intrigued."

Friends nicknamed Maguire "Army," for his neat appearance. An energetic young man with dark hair and a choirboy's face, a deep voice, and a machine-gun style of delivery, he had trained birds, baboons, chimps, capuchin monkeys, pigs, goats, dogs, camels, horses, ponies, llamas, large cats, cheetahs, lions, and tigers. He had worked for circuses, safari parks, and movie productions. Finding himself with nothing to do one afternoon, he had even taught his own pet shorthair cat how to meow on cue. But elephants were his specialty.

He had spent months studying them in Asia and Africa. By his own count he had trained sixty wild elephants, and he had saved the lives of many others by teaching them and their trainers how to get along. He believed that captives needed to be trained to know how to behave around humans. He based his confidence in his abilities on experience. He said that he had never failed at what he set out to do.

He told Carole, "I believe that God gave man dominion over all animals. The Bible says so. With that dominion comes a responsibility. Because of our intellect, we humans have a responsibility for the management of animals in our care. And that brings us to all the elephant questions you or your father are ever going to ask. You start 'em at the beginning, and they go to school properly, and when they grow up they don't smash people into walls and go running through gates."

"So you'll help my father," said Carole.

"I didn't say that," retorted Maguire. "I never worked for a cowboy before."

"They're no different from anybody else."

"Then I'll hear what he has to say."

A telephone conference was arranged. Neither Bob nor Maguire felt comfortable at first talking with each other. To

Maguire, Bob was an amateur who knew nothing about elephants; for Bob, Maguire was considering doing what Bob felt *he* should be doing, as one who knew animals better than most people and had trained horses for most of his adult life.

"Well, Mr. Norris," Maguire said on the phone, "I don't know. I don't know if I want to work for you or not."

Bob asked, "What's your problem?"

"Well, a lot of these guys have me come and work with them, and they start telling me how to train their elephant."

"Look, Mister, you know elephants. I don't. You know how to train them. I can train cutting horses, and I had a bear once. Elephants, I'm out of my class."

Maguire liked the sound of that. As Bob talked and he listened, he heard something else. He thought, You put a needy animal together with a man like Bob, and you get *magic*! That's what it is. Elephants are unlike any other animal. Anybody who spends any time around them will tell you that they are addictive because of their intellects and because of the interaction they have with humans. It is unique. It's not like a dog. You are dealing with a *brain*. I could tell by what Bob said that he was getting up in the morning and saying, "I can't *wait* to get down to the barn."

Bob told Maguire, "My wife and I want Amy to become a part of the ranch routine. I don't know where it will lead. I just want her trained so that I can go off and commune with her up by the water tanks. I don't care about tricks."

Maguire thought, He's already found a relationship with her. The level of commitment and understanding is what they give to each other. He said, "I can give you about thirty days and that's it. It'll cost you, though."

"How much?" asked Bob.

"Twelve thousand dollars, take it or leave it."

Bob said, "Holy cow!"

"Yes, sir."

"I guess we're talking about the laws of supply and demand here."

Said Maguire, "You bet we are."

As soon as he got off the phone, Bob called Carole, who said that Maguire's fee was her birthday present to him.

Bob told her, "Don't worry, honey. I'll take care of it. It's worth it to me. If she's not trained and she hurts someone, they'll call her 'out of control' and 'wild' and 'a rogue' elephant, and they'll kill her. I can't let that happen."

Weeks later Maguire piled out of his rented car at the ranch, ready to go. It took no more than a glance for him to see what he was up against: His student was a brat!

No wonder she needs training, he thought. It's not that she's wild; she's allowed to do anything she wants. He had never seen anything quite like her. Amy went where she wanted, when she wanted. She frisked people's pockets for treats. She explored their private parts with her trunk. She sniffed their faces and toyed with their hair. She played with

Michelle and Butch until she decided to stop. She obeyed no commands; she *knew* no commands. She knew no limits. As far as Maguire could tell, it was a miracle she hadn't already hurt someone.

Notwithstanding, he saw with his own eyes what he had sensed talking to Bob on the telephone. Bob and Amy enjoyed a unique relationship that was new in Maguire's experience with animals and people. He thought, Bob takes better care of Amy than 99 percent of people take care of their *children*. His goodwill just flows to her. There's something very special about him that will make my work a whole lot easier, even if she *is* a brat.

Where do we start?" Bob asked Maguire.

"With a talk, you and me."

"You're training her, not me."

"We'll see about that."

"Then what do you have to tell me?"

Maguire pointed to Amy. "She's wild. I think you should understand that. This animal is not a pet."

Bob looked at him hard. "Excuse me, but she's like my horse. We're partners. That's how I feel."

"But she *isn't* a horse, Mr. Norris. She's an elephant."

"What I mean to say—a lot of cowboys look at a horse like a pickup truck that takes them from point A to point B. They never reach down and pat it. When they're ropin' they never say, 'Good job, Buddy,' and scratch its back. When I'm out there with my horse, he's my partner, and that's how I look at Amy. She *is* just like my horse. Hell, she thinks she *is* a horse."

"I repeat, she is an elephant. Look with your own eyes."

"Listen, you're the trainer."

"Yes, I am," said Maguire.

"But I'm her friend. She's my little girl."

"By that you mean what?"

"I mean that you are not to hurt her, abuse her, or talk harshly to her in any way during her training. And none of that 'negative reinforcement' stuff either, not even with your voice. Take it or leave it. I'm paying you twelve thousand dollars. I want only the best."

Maguire had failed to get his meaning across. "I need a common language to train her with," he explained. "I have to work with *something* if this charm school is to succeed."

"It's up to you." Bob paused a second. "But I'm keeping my eye on you."

Right from the start, Amy wanted to please the teacher, though like a child on her first day at school, she had nerves. Bob and Michelle reassured her with their presence. The ranch hands watched by the fence. Michelle stayed close and seemed nervous too, as Amy began her first lesson.

Maguire, wearing jeans, a work shirt, and boots and carrying a long metal-tipped stick called an *ankus* at first confined Amy's movement with soft ropes tied to her legs and looped around her neck. He rewarded her with treats and words of encouragement when she did what he asked. He tapped her with the *ankus*; the hook, Maguire told Bob, represented the authority of the one giving the orders.

At first Amy associated the ropes, Bob thought, with her capture in Africa, with being chased, and with slaughter. Whatever the reason, she fought the ropes. She clearly did not like Maguire, who met her stubbornness with his own, until Amy came to see that he meant her no harm and would not let her have her own way.

The goal was to make her lie down on the command "Stretch out!" She clearly felt vulnerable lying down in front of Maguire. After constant repetition, however, she understood that she had nothing to fear. She probably wondered why Maguire asked her endlessly to lie down, then get up again, perhaps twenty times a training session. It was a tiring exercise for her. Maguire used her exhaustion to help her learn; the more tired, the more pliant she became as a student. He pulled her down with the ropes, then, on his command, let her get up again. She bellowed and cried, clearly with annoyance. As the days passed, she grew to understand what she was being asked to do. And she complied.

Next he taught her to pay attention with the command "Trunk Up!" Amy caught on and rolled her trunk back along her forehead and raised her head to receive a "monkey biscuit" treat in her open mouth. A loudly spoken "All right!"

Bob and Amy out for a trot.

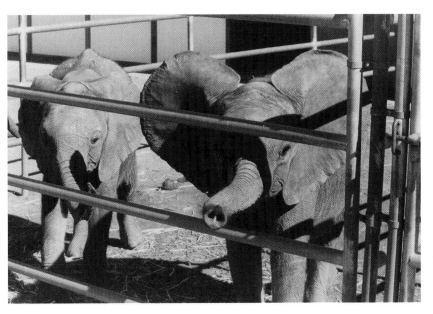

Amy hanging out with a friend.

Bath time!

Bob and Amy relaxing in the shade.

Amy battling with some branches.

Amy and Larry come out to play.

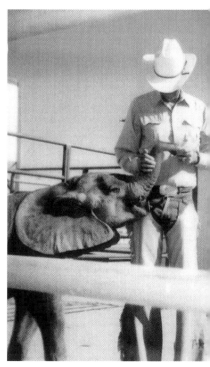
A present from Amy.

Amy playing with a friend.

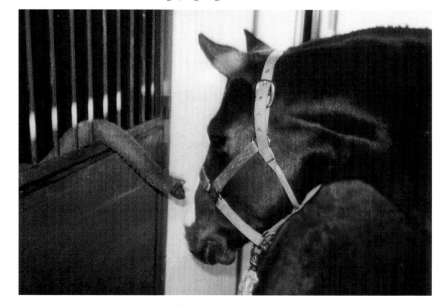

Amy shares a secret with Bob.

Bob plants a big one on Amy.

Bob, Amy, and America the Beautiful.

Randall Moore with his elephant in Botswana.

LEFT: Buck deVries

BELOW: Bob, Jane, and Buckles with Amy in the back.

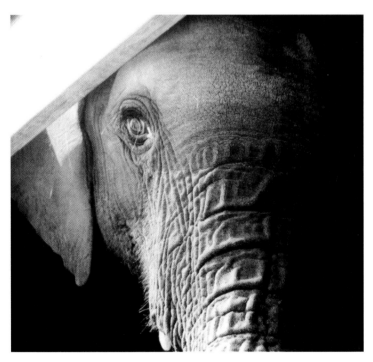

With a tear running down from her eye, a very sad Amy is loaded onto a van heading to Florida from Bobby's ranch in Texas.

signaled her to relax. She lifted her leg at the knee; and she turned in the directions that Maguire asked her to.

"Damn, she's mellow," he told Bob, when Amy flopped on the ground without being told.

Watching him work over several days, Bob grew to like Maguire. The feeling was returned. The two men, one old enough to be the other's father, had more than Amy in common. They shared a love of animals and talked late at night, always about animals. For the first time Bob could discuss his passion with someone who understood Amy and knew all about elephants.

One afternoon Maguire and Bob visited the local zoo to see what zoos were like for elephants. Maguire had nothing against them, though some zoos bothered him, and the local zoo was one of them. He pointed out to Bob the lone elephant that stood on a sun-baked concrete pad with a bucket of water and only a pile of hay for feed. She had no companion, not even a pet chicken or goat. She rocked back and forth out of boredom, hitting her trunk against a steel door.

"And people wonder why they turn rogue," said Maguire. "That animal is lost. Just look at her."

Bob was shocked. "Are the zoos all like this?" he asked Maguire.

"No, thank goodness."

"I'd never want that for Amy," Bob said.

"It doesn't have to be," Maguire told him.

The next morning Bob was helping Maguire. After a particularly strenuous session, he asked for a recess. He wiped the sweat off his brow with his sleeve.

"Army, something's wrong," he told him.

"What do you mean?"

"You say to her, 'Amy, down.' Then I got to pull her down with the rope here. You're getting paid, and I'm doing all the work."

Maguire said, "That's because I'm the teacher."

"And Amy's the pupil."

"No, that's where you're wrong, Mr. Norris. *You're* the pupil."

At the end of about thirty days, Army *and* Bob had taught Amy as much etiquette as she was ever going to learn.

The cowhands came to Amy's graduation ceremony, as did Carole and, of course, Maguire and Jane, and Amy's veterinarian, Laura Harris, who arrived dressed as if for a party. Bob's stallion Big Bob wore a dress saddle. Michelle and Butch wandered around looking for handouts. Bob's grandson's elementary school class filled the bleachers of the ranch's indoor showring, usually used for horse sales.

Over to one side, Jane was chatting with an invited member of the local press.

"Is Bob proud of Amy? My, *yes!* Ask him about all the pictures of her that he carries in his back pocket. Any time we go to a dinner party, he pulls out his Amy photos. He passes them around like she was his granddaughter."

What Jane did not say was that their friends were so

accustomed to being shown photos of Amy that whenever Bob pulled out his wallet they groaned, "Here he goes again!"

For this occasion Bob dressed in a spiffy Western outfit—clean jeans, a cotton-candy colored shirt with fringe and pearl snap buttons, a colorful bandanna, and a clean, nearly new hat. He wore a belt with the big gold-etched oval buckle of the National Cutting Horse Association. Astride Big Bob, he entered the ring with Amy. The applause echoed off the metal roof.

Now Amy was attentive, watchful, and measured. She had a purpose, which was to obey Bob and Maguire. And she even seemed proud of her training. She began her "graduation exercise" as she'd been taught: With Bob and Big Bob at her side, she followed a series of routine movements. She skipped on alternate front feet in what Bob described to his audience as "break-dancing." She waved a little American parade flag in her trunk. Next Bob handed her a handkerchief, which she waved in imitation of Iraqi troops' surrender in the recent Gulf War.

Bob walked beside her around the ring and up close to the bleachers, where the children could touch her when she stretched her trunk toward them. Bob hummed the *Star-Spangled Banner*, and Amy stood at attention on an elevated stand.

Watching from the bleachers, Maguire told T. J., "She likes the limelight. My God, she's a ham."

Bob addressed the children in the audience, "You kids

take naps?" Without waiting for a reply, he told Amy, "Stretch out!" but she looked at him and, apparently unprepared to take a nap, just walked away.

Now Bob was uncertain. He was powerless to stop her from doing anything she wanted, in spite of her training. In her own time, however, to Bob's relief, she returned to him, and then she finally lay down for "a nap." Feeling more confident, Bob reached his hand into a carpenter's apron he had tied around his waist for a "treat," and popped a cookie into her mouth. Amy stood up again, and Bob draped a bright pink corsage on a long ribbon around her neck and gave her a scrolled "diploma" as proof of her graduation.

"She learned at school, and it wasn't always easy," he told the kids. "Cowboys and their elephants *stand apart.*"

Amy blew on an oversize harmonica, while Bob sang off-key, *"The eyes of Texas are upon you, all the live long day."* He took off his hat and waved to the audience. "I just want to tell you folks, and you kids too, that Amy here, this little girl of mine, has come through what most of us never could. She never complained. She did it on her own, and she had a lot more to overcome than a lot of people. She is an example of what *we* can do, if we care to. I want you to know I'm proud of Amy."

Laura Harris stood at one side of the ring. Observing Bob and Amy together, she thought, Amy's temperament is sunny due to the rapture of Bob. It's just that simple. There are animals with good personalities and difficult personalities, the same as people. There are those that have had hard times and easy times, like people too. The point of it is that Amy has found happiness with Bob. All the rest is in the past. Bob is her reality, and she thrives in it. She's happy at last, and that's that.

CHAPTER FIVE

n the days that followed, Amy picked up where she had left off before her training—doing exactly what she wanted, where and when the spirits moved her.

Bob had looked forward to her companionship when he rode up to the water tank, where he sometimes went to commune with nature. He liked the idea of having her to talk to, but Amy could not be persuaded to go. She liked her paddock and stayed near her stall, her toys and wallow, and the bales of alfalfa stacked near the barn.

One morning Bob rode out the driveway on Big Bob, with Butch and Jo trailing along. He looked back over his shoulder. Amy was following him with a tentative step. He did not try to hide his pleasure. He continued to the outbuildings near the wallow. Amy stopped. She turned back slowly, and Bob rode on.

That afternoon when Bob got back to the barn, a stranger was standing by a truck with the official insignia of the U.S. Department of Agriculture (USDA). The inspector was dressed in black rubber boots and a faded green zippered jumpsuit and he carried a clipboard. Bob tipped his hat in greeting. The inspector told him that he had come about Amy.

"What's your business with elephants?" Bob wanted to know.

"The Department of Agriculture is mandated to make sure that elephants are being treated properly, the ones in zoos and circuses and ones like yours. Not many like yours, though."

"Well, how did you hear about me? I haven't advertised the fact she's here."

"The man who sold her to you."

"Jackson?"

"I guess that's his name. The law required him to report the buyer to us." He referred to his clipboard. "I'm here to check around the ranch to make sure of the elephant's safety."

"She's safe," said Bob. "You can take my word for it."

"It's the *law*," the inspector said.

"Well, do what you have to," Bob told him, a little disgusted at the interference.

He watched him go over Amy's stall inch by inch. With a tape measure he measured the diameter of the pipe fence of her paddock, the square footage of her paddock and stall, the proximity of electrical lines, and so on. His attention to detail amazed Bob. Some of what he observed passed the Department of Agriculture's guidelines, but not all—The electrical outlets and overhead electrical lines, for instance, were conceivably within reach of Amy's trunk.

On his rounds the inspector told Bob that some private owners treated their elephants inhumanely. Indeed, they kept them in such terrible conditions that they had forced the government to intervene. They locked them in dark barns, never cleaned their quarters, fed them poorly, and kept them chained to the ground night and day. Bob winced. He began to understand the USDA's purpose. He even came to see that the inspector had valuable knowledge to impart about elephants. By the end of his tour, Bob told him, "I'd rather you were overcautious."

"Some of their owners don't know what these animals are capable of. They can hurt themselves just out of their curiosity." He pointed out to Bob things that he needed to change.

"She's screwing around all the time," Bob told the man. "If there is anything to get into, she'll get into it, just like a kid with no idea of the dangers. She walks into my tack room and starts messin' around with my equipment. You always have to be very careful. I am; I try to be. You can't let her get into the feed room, either, or she'll eat too much and then get colic." He told the inspector, "Knock on wood, we've never had a sick day with her once she got over the shock of what happened in Africa."

The inspector said he would be back. "The government has the authority to confiscate the animal for its own protection," he warned Bob, if the changes were not made.

Bob had no intention of losing Amy to government rules. But he wondered whether this man's unscheduled visit was not the thin end of a wedge. How much did the government see ownership of an elephant as being unnatural, and therefore, how much would they continue to meddle in his private affairs?

Now that she was trained, Bob expected Amy to help with the chores.

"What do you give an elephant to do?" T. J. asked Bob one day.

"Darned if I know," Bob replied, looking at Amy in the paddock.

T. J. thought for several minutes. "She could do tricks."

"No, that's fake," said Bob. "I want her to make a difference around here. We're not running a circus."

"She could take care of the colts."

"Yes, and the cows."

T. J. laughed. "She could be like a *cowgirl*."

"And do a cowgirl's work too," said Bob. "That's what we'll do."

Soon after the decision was made, Bob was trying to

teach Amy by example how to cut cattle with her size and with her trunk. She should have been superior at cutting cows to any horse. With that thought in mind, Bob took her into the pen with eight or nine young steers that huddled in a bunch in a far corner, facing out, their eyes bulging with the usual fear. They hardly noticed Bob on Big Bob. When one of them moved, as cows will, they all moved in a tight group.

The trick of cutting was to cut one cow out from this bunch. On the open range each cow was caught, branded, and medicated. Cows were semiwild animals and did not like to do what the cowboys wanted them to. Bob could cut the cows elegantly on horseback. He began to show Amy what he wanted her to do, but she seemed distracted and did not pay attention. Cows were objects to play with, she seemed to believe. Bob could have sworn that the cows' terror amused her.

A good cutting horse cuts steers even without a rider to guide it. Almost by instinct a horse will feint left and right, shifting its weight, trying to commit the cow to a direction.

Bob got down from Big Bob and walked over to Amy. He ordered her to "stretch out!" He was carrying his *ankus*, and she obeyed him. Bob ran his gloved hand along her back. He talked to her, and he threw a horse blanket on the small of her back. He reached into the pocket of his carpenter's apron for a treat. "Good Amy," he told her. He said, "Trunk up!" She was curious and watched to see what he would do next.

He did the unexpected. In a quick move he straddled her back with his legs. "All right," he told her. He waited; she waited. They stood in one place. Elephant and rider both seemed to have expected a different response. Amy looked around at him on her back and reached over her own head for a treat. "Move up, Amy," he told her. She stepped forward, and they circled the pen at a slow walk.

Over the next few days, however, Bob felt that something about his training was just not right. Amy could cut steers almost as well as a horse. But increasingly he felt that this kind of work was beneath her dignity. Elephants were not designed to anticipate the motion of a frightened calf. Amy had a trunk to help her, and she was willing to go along with what Bob asked her to do. But in Bob's eyes she was too noble an animal for a man to ride her like a horse. In spite of her training he still wanted to preserve her untamed nature and beauty as an animal. He never asked her to carry him again.

He chose instead to teach her how to walk the colts. He handed her their lead rope and said, "Take it, Amy." She already knew how to unlatch and open the paddock gate. He taught her to block the colts with her body from running past her. She reached out her trunk, collected their leads and pulled them up tight, and then walked them back out of the gate. Soon Bob didn't even tell her what to do. She seemed to enjoy her work.

She followed Bob everywhere and complained loudly when he entered his office and shut the door. She waited for him and her patience often amazed Bob, who could hear her grumble on the other side of the closed door. She was happily excited when he came out, greeting him with a kiss on the face and a frisk of his clothes.

She was still cautious about wandering too far away from her paddock and stall, even with Bob by her side. The paddock was her home and represented the fulfillment of the important needs of food, water, and shelter. The paddock was where her toys were scattered and where she knew to find Michelle. Bob had long ago given up asking her to ride the fences with him. He went out alone on Big Bob, with Butch and Jo trotting along beside him.

Fence riding was a rancher's chore, as old as the invention of barbed wire. A cow that went through the ranch fence was a lost cow, and lost revenue to the rancher. Since cows on the range tended to follow the leader, one lost cow often meant more. Besides, a busy interstate highway ran along the eastern boundary of Bob's T Cross ranch, carrying trucks and automobiles at high speeds twenty-four hours a day.

For a cowboy fence riding was relaxing and could even be fun in good weather. The chore called for long, solitary sojourns under a big sky. For Bob it was a time for reflection, singing songs, and talking to his horse and himself, while keeping an eye out for wire breaks and broken posts.

Usually when he was setting out, Amy walked behind him and Big Bob as far as her wallow before turning back. Bob no longer looked around to see if she was following him.

But one fine day, for a reason known only to Amy, before she seemed to notice how far she had gone past the wallow, she was out of sight of the barns and ranch buildings. She looked back, and then, with a snort of determination, she followed Bob, who slowed up to her pace. He lowered his hat and watched her out of the corner of his eye.

She explored around rocks and under bushes. Lizards and strange ground-nesting birds and rabbits burst from under the sage. The wind whipped in gusts, blowing tumbleweeds as big as beach balls across her path. She chased after them with Butch and Jo. Her curiosity astounded Bob, who was already aware of her inquisitive nature. Once she stood still looking up at the scudding clouds. Bob watched her, realizing that she had not lived in the wild like this since Africa. Now, like a child ordered to go outside to play against her will, Amy was apparently having fun. She browsed, sniffed, and listened to the sounds of calling birds. She picked up sticks and burned cactus plants, uprooted rocks, and root-bound tufts of grasses.

Bob grew to believe that Amy could appreciate beauty. She paused to sniff the light fragrance of a wildflower in bloom, and she seemed to take notice of the brilliance of a buttercup. She watched the cloud formations. She plucked out of the air the windblown fluff of cottonwood trees. She held new leaves on the fingers of her trunk. She watched flocks of wild ducks and geese fly by. Small creatures that scurried out from under the inquiry of her trunk amused her.

Bob thought that she even smiled and believed that he heard the sounds of her laughter.

From the highway, passengers in cars spied her along the fence, some of them blinking in disbelief. The cars usually drove on for a short distance. Bob sometimes counted to three, waiting for the car's brake lights to go on. The passengers turned their heads and watched Bob and Amy with their mouths wide open. They really *had* seen an elephant. The drivers pulled over on the shoulder of the road and reversed to the point where Bob, Amy, and the dogs were walking on the other side of the fence.

Bob was too much of a showman not to give people a closer look at her. Sometimes the roadside turned into an impromptu audience of excited children, dogs, cats, and parents. Most of them had seen elephants before at the circus or in a zoo. But none had ever been found on a cow ranch with a cowboy.

The parents often asked Bob excited questions, while the kids reached through the strands of barbed wire to touch Amy. Bob gave the children treats to give her, and Amy frisked their pockets for whatever else she could find.

They often returned from riding the fences hot and tired. Bob sometimes pointed the nozzle of a hose at Amy to cool her down. She wriggled, groaned, and turned in circles. Bob rubbed her skin with a long-handled brush and she backed into him, as if to tell him, *More there*, that's *the itchy spot*! She then finished at a ten-foot-high mound of sawdust dumped there for her to roll in. She lay down on her side like a puppy and scratched her back in the dust, while Bob heaped sawdust on her stomach with a coal shovel.

Once, after a hot summer fence ride when the thermometer on the barn read 108 degrees, Bob was sweating through his shirt, and a band of sweat stained his hat by the time they got back to the ranch. Amy ran around the corner of the barn. It was too hot for him to run after her, and besides, he thought, she was probably going to find shade. He was unsaddling Big Bob when Amy came back around the corner. She walked up to him, raised her trunk, and sprayed him all over with water she had drawn from a tub. Then she went back for a second trunk and cooled herself with its spray.

T. J. was watching. "Is that what I think it is?" he asked Bob. "She is such a little mother."

As time went by Amy and Bob lived and worked side by side, Amy's uniqueness was long past almost anyone noticing. She was one of the crew. When Bob worked his horses in the cutting pen, she worked along with him. Each day was just another day. Bob by now had put away his video camera. The photos of Amy did not come out of his wallet so often. Amy had become part of the ranch's normal routine.

The relationship between her and Bob seemed perfect for itself alone, not for what it should or could have been in some ideal world. It was an odd affection and respect, Bob liked to think, between two species that connected on a level no one could really explain. Bob enjoyed Amy, and she seemed to enjoy him, and that was enough. They couldn't talk, but their intuitions sufficed as a language, like an old married couple long past needing to explain.

Still, Bob was never entirely certain if his affection for her was requited. Then one morning, after Amy had been at the ranch nearly three years, she offered him a gift as rare as anything a human ever has received from an elephant. He was in her stall when she raised her head and took his hand by her trunk and put it in her mouth. Bob told himself, Either she wants to eat my hand or she wants me to stroke her tongue. Amy, her eyes half-closed, gave a low rumble like a purr.

Bob guessed that she was telling him in her own way that she accepted him into *her* species. In human terms he was her family, and she would live here as she was meant to in Africa. Bob felt happy knowing that from now on she would never be anything less than healthy, happy, and strong. Words failed him, except to say, "I guess everything came together for Amy at that moment."

They had picnics together under the eucalyptus trees. The air was clear, the wildflowers were in bloom, and the whole summer lay ahead. Amy stood at one end of a picnic table and Michelle at the other. Butch stretched out in the shade.

Bob tuned a radio to a country music station and put the volume down low. He took their lunches from a paper bag and spread the food out on the table, and they ate together.

Sometimes the air around Amy shook with vibrations. Was she trying to communicate with him? If so, he felt sorry for her. She understood him, but when she sent him messages, if that's what the vibrations were, he had no idea what she was trying to say. Often she felt his moods before he did. When he was sad, angry, down, or happy, she adjusted to his mood. In the mornings when he was feeling good, she greeted him with excited trumpetings. When he was down, she was always quiet and watchful. She seemed to pout with him, and she knew unerringly when he was leaving her for the day. When he returned to the barn, her trunk went up, her mouth opened, and she trumpeted what Bob interpreted as a hello. She plugged him with a kiss on his face, and he blew into the end of her trunk, greeting her as Army Maguire had told him elephants do.

In the spring the cowboys rounded up the pregnant cows and early calves. Bob and Amy rode "bog" to rescue those stuck in watering holes, with a rope around the saddle horn. Sometimes he waded in after them, while Amy held Big Bob's reins. With her strength Amy could have pulled the cows out of the mud with her trunk. But sometimes the cows freed *themselves* at the very sight of her.

"They'd walk on water just seeing her approach them," Bob said.

The cowboys kept the herds moving. On a ranch like the T Cross, cows behaved like a huge mowing machine that had to be shifted from one section to another to prevent over-grazing. After a severe winter the hands brought the cows cottonseed cake and hay. After mild winters, they grazed and fattened until spring roundup. The ranch hands and Bob cut and branded the calves, then let them loose to roam the ranch for the summer period of fattening. The work was hard on man and beast, and the days were long, even for Amy, who was assigned no particular chores except to stay out of the way. Her presence had a strange effect on the steers. When she was there, they watched her and were easier to cut. She stayed close to Bob, as if she had assigned herself the role of his bodyguard. Otherwise no one paid much attention to her, except to tell her to move out of the way.

Bob enjoyed Amy's sense of humor. He knew as certainly as he knew what made *him* laugh that she laughed at the cows, and the colts made her trumpet at different intensities of sound that Bob was certain were giggles. She even seemed to understand the pathos of Michelle fretting over being left alone. Amy, Bob believed, thought of the goat as a sweet simpleton. Amy teased her, closed gates on her, and sprayed her with the garden hose, she pushed her into the mud and threw toys at her. Michelle seemed unfazed and only wanted to be with her friend Amy.

In the summers Bob and Amy invented games to play. In one he ignored her until she complained to him with grumbles, moans, and trumpeting. He chased her. Her ears spread wide, her trunk stretched straight out, and she trumpeted. The chase ended with Bob spraying her with water from the hose and Amy spraying him with her trunk.

In the mornings they often played hide and seek. Cleaning out her stall with a shovel and a push broom, Bob told Amy to get out of her stall—there was hardly room for her *and* him. Reluctantly she went into the paddock, but she was back a minute later, trying to stuff herself in.

"No, Amy," he told her.

She inched her toe over the threshold. Bob told her with mock seriousness, "No, no."

She pulled her foot back. Then, little by little, she inched it forward again. Bob was convinced that she thought of herself as tiny, even invisible. Now she put in her other foot and then her shoulders, until she was back in and the stall was crowded again. Bob blustered with comic indignation, and Amy fled down the barn gallery "like Big Bird," Bob said, with her ears straight out to the sides, trumpeting and moving her legs in her "silly walk" of loose and disjointed limbs, trunk and flopping ears.

Once out of the barn she turned back into the paddock and came around to the outside of her stall. She released the catch on the lower door with her trunk and softly stepped back into the stall. Bob was waiting. He scolded her, and she ran off again, honking and bellowing.

This time around, as she circled through the paddock, Bob would hide himself in another stall, squatting down in the corner by the gallery door. Amy looked in her stall; he wasn't there! She searched the barn, trumpeting with excitement. She *knew* where he was hiding: He chose the same stall to hide in each time. And when she discovered him squatting in the corner, she trumpeted louder and ran away with an excitement and joy that Bob knew were just that, no matter what behaviorists said about animals being incapable of such feelings.

In the late mornings when the sun was warm, Bob sometimes napped by the paddock fence. He'd rest one boot on the rail, tilt back on the rear legs of a straight-back chair, and tip his hat down low over his brow. Amy was usually in the paddock playing with Butch and Michelle, and she'd wander over to Bob, who'd take his foot off the rail and put it on the ground. The game for Amy, Bob believed, was to see how close she could come to stepping on his foot without actually doing it. She went past, then around the paddock again, and again and again.

Bob watched her from under the brim of his hat. One morning a young horse that was "goofy and couldn't concentrate on anything" stood looking at Amy's hay in front of her stall door. Amy had backed up to Bob, and he was scratching her rump. The radio was playing. The colt entered the paddock and walked over to Amy's hay. Reins looped over his neck held his head from the hay. While Bob was watching her, Amy looked at the colt. She looked back at Bob as if to say, *Excuse me for a minute*. She went over to the colt, led him out of her paddock by the reins, and closed the gate. Amy then walked over, picked up a big trunkful of her hay, and walked back to the gate. She held out the food and fed the colt like a mother with a baby. She went back for more and fed him again.

Bob pushed back his hat. He thought, God, where's my camera?

Bob's favorite local restaurant was El Chorro's, a relaxed, al fresco place with a patio and tables under wide colored umbrellas. It had a bar that stocked numerous tequilas, and two small dining rooms with big windows, daylight streaming through their panes. El Chorro's served Mexican food. Sometimes in the mornings Bob ordered *huevos rancheros* and sticky buns baked fresh in the restaurant's ovens.

One day around brunch he drove up with Amy in a horse trailer. Amy stepped out at valet parking as Bob waved hello to the owner, Joe Miller. For something to do, while the patrons on the patio watched, Amy raised her trunk, waved a napkin, and performed her "break dance." As a reward the owner served her a platter of sticky buns from the kitchen.

Miller asked Bob, "What's a cowboy doing with an elephant?"

"Having fun!"

"With an *elephant*?"

"Hell, why not? Like we say, 'If you're not having fun you're not living right.' "

From her knowing how to "play" an oversize plastic harmonica, Bob soon resolved that Amy had an ear for music. Like a stage mother, he decided to nurture her talent with piano lessons. He consulted with the experts at Toys "R" Us and came home with an electric piano keyboard in the back of his truck.

He set up the piano in Amy's paddock. She was curious and tested the keys with her trunk. Bob sliced a carrot. Amy loved carrots almost as much as sticky buns, and Bob placed a slice on a piano key. As she picked up the carrot, she pushed on the key, and a single note sounded.

"Hold it. Hold it. Hold it. Steady. . . . Hold that down." Bob waited, then told her, "All right!" and she ate the carrot on the key. Then another note, and so on, until finally she understood what he wanted from her. Bob told T. J., "She'll never make a melody, but I can't make one either."

She played, and Bob occasionally danced. The ranch hands, watching their boss scuffle in the dirt, wandered over, wondering whether he had gone loco. Dancing to Amy's tune on the piano, he told his hands, "This, boys, is a Zimbabwe

tune that you may not recognize." Soon they too were dancing in the dirt, slapping their chaps, waving their hats, and
laughing loud enough to be heard out on the highway. Bob
sang along to her music, beat time, and waved his arms like
an orchestra conductor. Seeing the hands and Bob shuffling
in the dirt, Amy danced too, and with the touch of a control
button on the piano Bob switched the play to automatic. To
the sounds of Disney's "It's A Small World," he danced and
Amy shuffled her feet, and the dust rose up in a cloud.

Amy basked in the attention of an audience. Bob believed
that the discipline and the exercise of "performance"
engaged her mind. By the standards of what circus elephants were trained to do, her "act" was nothing more than
what elephants *naturally* do.

His brunch with Amy at El Chorro's gave Bob another
idea. Amy's little act had entertained the guests, so why not
set up an act for kids to enjoy? Bob and Jane gave generously to charities out of a sense of duty and obligation to
those who were less fortunate. But giving, Bob thought, was
never as good as *doing* for others.

One morning he drove Amy in the horse trailer to a
local Colorado Springs public elementary school. When he
stepped out of his truck he was dressed in a red cowboy
shirt with fringed sleeves that Jane had patterned for him.
Amy backed out of the trailer, followed by Michelle, Big Bob,
and Butch. A local TV station had sent a reporter with a
camera crew to film Amy's performance.

Amy and Bob walked from the parking lot to the school's baseball diamond, where the children were waiting in the bleachers. Amy did not need to do anything but be herself. A real live elephant has amazing powers of enchantment over children. Bob set up her electric piano and rolled out a steel tub. Amy, with Michelle behind her, wandered to the baseball diamond's home plate, which she tried to pry out of the ground. The children screamed with delight. Amy carried the rubber rectangle up to the pitcher's mound, dropped it in the dirt, then tried to excavate the pitcher's "rubber." Already, before the show even began, she was the star!

When she finally began her act, she turned to the bleachers and bowed on her knee. She waved an American flag in her trunk and played the piano. Bob sang "The Yellow Rose of Texas" and kept up a running monologue about Amy's history and as much as he knew about elephants in the wild. The children cheered when Amy perched on the steel tub and hopped in her "break dance," and when she rolled over on her side. She blew on the harmonica as a finale and took bows as the children clapped their hands.

That evening Amy appeared on the TV station's news. And soon after, invitations to perform arrived in the ranch's mailbox. Bob was flattered. He told Jane, "We're getting known, I guess."

One of the first invitations Bob accepted was a charity dinner in town. The party's theme was "Carousel Caravan," with drinks, dinner, and dancing, under the stars. A buffet table stretched from one end of a long white tent to the other, covered with chafing dishes and platters. Guests wore the costumes of circus performers—sideshow acts, lion tamers, high-wire walkers, clowns, and so on.

Bob arrived with Amy in the trailer when the party was in full swing. The professional organizer of the evening, who did not know Bob and thought of him as a hired entertainer, gave him a welcoming look that said *Carnie* and *Avoid!* As he was unloading Amy from the trailer, the woman told him, "Now, if you are hungry you can go over there to eat with the other help."

"I won't be talked to like that," said Bob.

"Oh, yes you will."

He pointed to the buffet table. "I'll eat with all those other folks over there."

"No, you won't!"

"Why the heck not?"

She stared at him with contempt. "Because you are not wearing a costume."

Bob knew when to seize an opportunity. He went along to charity benefits because of Jane, not because he enjoyed the chitchat, and now was his chance to escape back to the ranch. He smiled at the lady, tipped his hat, packed Amy into the trailer and delivered her back to the barn. He settled her in, watering and feeding her, and he then drove to El Chorro's for dinner, leaving the restaurant with a bag of sticky buns for Amy's breakfast.

From then on Bob accepted many invitations, including one date in Denver at the Western National Stock Show and Rodeo. The guests were seated on hay bales and in folding chairs set out in a horseshoe. They ate off paper plates in their laps. Amy went through her paces but she was distracted, and she missed her cues. Bob wondered if she needed a break from performing. He asked her to sit on the tub, and she paused. Bob thought, *Uh-oh.* She was looking straight at a man sitting in the front row with a full paper plate in his lap, of boiled corn, chicken, and barbecued beans. Amy snapped out her trunk and in an instant snatched his plate away. The man fell over backward in surprise, and while the audience laughed, Bob decided that he should retire her for a while from showbiz.

He got out of bed one morning, and his old football knee locked up. He hated to admit that he needed to see a doctor—cowboys resented sick spells more than five-mile walks. At Jane's urging he went to an orthopedic surgeon who scoped his knee. For the next few weeks, back at the ranch, he hobbled around on crutches. Jane worried for him. "What if you can't move out of her way and Amy bumps into you by accident?" she wanted to know.

"Then it's my own damn fault."

He went straight to the barn on crutches and opened Amy's stall door and Amy, clearly glad to see him, walked into the barn gallery and put the end of her trunk all over his face. Bob hobbled down the gallery to the tack room, and she came along. He looked over and laughed. Amy was hobbling with the same jerky rhythm of him on his crutches.

"Knock it off!" he told her. "I won't be made fun of by an elephant!"

CHAPTER SIX

Amy had lived at the ranch for five years when Bob and Jane became regular "snowbirds" during the winters, fleeing Colorado for the warmth of Phoenix. They packed up to leave after the fall roundup, with Bob turning over T Cross to a manager. And with a horse trailer hitched to the pickup and loaded with their menagerie, Bob, with Jane beside him in the cab, turned onto Route 25 for the drive south through Pueblo toward the New Mexico border near Trinidad.

Bob had customized the horse trailer to accommodate Amy, and for space to carry Jane's dresses and jewelry and Bob's saddles and bridles. Bales of hay were tied on top. The trailer groaned under the weight of Amy, Michelle, Big Bob and usually another horse of Bob's choice, the two dogs, plus Amy's piano, which he put within her reach to play as they drove.

The night before setting out, Bob checked the Weather Channel on TV for conditions over the Raton Pass, just out of Trinidad, where the temperatures often dropped to freezing. The bodies of the other animals in the trailer helped to keep Amy warm. But one fall, as they were driving at eight to nine thousand feet south of Raton, a whiteout blizzard came up that frightened Bob. He stopped, bundled Amy in blankets, and drove fast through the storm until they reached Albuquerque, where they turned west on Interstate 40.

"What're you hauling?" a trucker asked Bob over his CB radio.

"Horses," he replied on his CB.

"Funny-lookin' horse you got there, cowboy."

"Why did you say that?"

"I saw a trunk come out the side."

"Oh, that's my elephant."

Soon thereafter, a convoy of 18-wheelers often lined up behind the trailer, waiting to pass by and look at Amy, who trumpeted in reply to the blasts of their air horns.

When they stopped for gas, Amy naturally wanted to get out of the trailer and stretch her legs. A station attendant, filling the tank with gas, asked Bob what he was hauling.

"An elephant."

"Oh, yeah, sure."

"If you don't believe me, open the door and look for yourself."

Amy stepped out down past the attendant, who was too frightened to move. Ignoring him, she wandered around the station's platform, attempting to frisk the Coke and candy vending machines. Bob tried to lead her back into the trailer, but she would not be rushed. A crowd soon gathered; Jane tensed as some children walked right up to Amy. Bob enlisted a posse from the garage, who helped to push her back into the trailer. Bob never again asked anyone to "see for themselves."

He laughed as they drove off, but the incident worried Jane, who told him, "Things like that, I mean—Amy might be like a big dog but she *isn't* a big dog. What if she had hurt one of those children?"

At first Bob had been able to keep Amy out of sight. But the inspectors on the border at the State of Arizona's agricultural and animal port of entry near Gallup, New Mexico, could not be fooled for long. On their initial trips together from Colorado to Arizona, Bob often stayed with the trailer, while T. J., who came along to help with the animals, went inside the station. The inspector asked him what kind of livestock they were hauling over the border into Arizona that day. T. J. glanced out the window. The trailer was parked in plain sight: Bob was bribing Amy with carrots to keep her trunk in the trailer.

"Equine or bovine?" the inspector asked.

"Cows," T. J. replied.

The inspector looked at the form. T. J. looked out the window. He gasped—Amy's trunk was waving in the air in plain view. Bob was bent over, giggling.

The inspector saw T. J.'s horrified gaze. He asked him, "Why's your truck squattin' so low?"

T. J. smoothed his mustache. The trailer was slanted on one side, and every time Amy took a step from one side of the trailer to the other, it tilted. He said, "Horses. They all go over to one side, then the other."

"Okay, then. Have a nice trip."

Back on the road, T. J. turned to Bob. "*Never* do that to me again."

Bob smiled. "Tell that to Amy."

She could do nothing about her size. She was almost six years old and getting big. She now weighed nearly two thousand pounds and stood five feet tall at the center of her back. She had a few thousand pounds of weight yet to put on, and a couple of feet to grow in her lifetime: Elephants continued to grow their whole lives.

"They *do*?" Bob asked, surprised, when Maguire told him that part of the elephant life cycle.

"And Africans like her get bigger than Indians," Maguire said.

At the time, Bob could hardly visualize what Maguire described, but now he was starting to see it for real.

As Amy grew, the trailer became for Bob an instrument of doubt: He wanted to ignore the proof of her size. She was turning seven, and though she had grown up for everyone else, she was still Bob's "little girl," no matter that nothing at all about her was little anymore.

He accommodated her size in an effort to ignore it. He removed the horses from her trailer on the trips from Colorado. That worked until the trailer started to wobble and strain at the hitch with her increasing weight. Bob now had to grasp the steering wheel with tight fists just to keep the truck and trailer on the road.

"When she moves, sometimes the whole damn truck shifts," he told T. J.

"I can see that," replied T. J., who often followed the trailer in a car.

"I can compensate with the steering wheel and the brakes. I can get used to the movement and the sway. It's a weird sensation, though, knowing you can't stop fast or you'll whack her up. You have to think ahead about all the things that could happen."

T. J. nodded, doubting that Bob was even capable of thinking ahead where Amy was concerned. He was simply blind to everything about her except his affection for her.

At the Arizona port of entry she finally became impossible to hide anymore. She was simply too big to take across without the complications of explaining why, the endless paperwork, and the prohibitions. On one trip an inspector looked up from the forms on the counter.

"You state here that you got two horses with you," he said to Bob. "What the hell you need two rigs for to haul two of 'em?"

"Well, we need the extra trailer for the stock," Bob stretched the truth.

The inspector looked out the window at Amy's trunk waving in the air—outside her trailer. Her head bumped up against the ceiling. Even a numbskull could have seen that she was an elephant.

He looked startled. "What the hell's that?"

"What?" asked Bob with feigned surprise.

The inspector pointed out the window. "That!"

Bob said, "A cow."

The inspector looked at him real hard.

"A horse," Bob said, changing his mind.

"A horse with a damned trunk?"

Bob grinned slyly. "It takes all kinds."

"Well, cowboy, whatever it is you got in there, get it out of here before I impound it."

Jane watched all this with growing dismay, until one day, despite herself, she had to ask Bob, "What are we going to do?"

"About what?" He knew what. "Something will turn up to fix it," he told her.

"Nothing is going to fix her size. She's an elephant, Bob."

Yes, of course, but Amy was also his *friend*.

"Can't we leave her at T Cross when we go to Arizona?" Jane asked.

"And who would take care of her there? Who would be responsible for her?"

After a long silence, Bob stopped on the shoulder of the road. He got out of the truck and got into Amy's trailer. He sat with his back to the wall. He talked to her as a friend. He felt sad and did not hide his feelings behind a cheerful voice. The time was fast approaching for some decision that would change their lives. Amy was growing up, and Bob had choices to make. Damn, he thought. I don't even want to *think* about what to do.

The Arizona "snowbird" life mirrored on a smaller scale what Bob and Jane had built for themselves in Colorado. They owned a nice house in the Paradise Valley suburb of Scottsdale, and Bob maintained a miniranch for Amy and his horses and a few cows on the outskirts of Phoenix, by the canal.

With Bob's constant presence and encouragement, Amy adapted to Arizona during her months there each year. Her stall and paddock were about the same size and shape as they were in Colorado. She ate the same foods and had the company of Michelle and the cowdogs. Best of all, now that he was away from the big Colorado ranch, Bob spent the whole day with her, every day. They walked the ranch's fences, and they wandered over to the canal and watched the water flow by. The skies were a sulfurous yellow and the air was hot; gray rabbits and sometimes an armadillo wandered in from the desert; the nights were cool and the stars bright.

In the 1990s, few places in the United States were growing faster than Phoenix and Scottsdale. It was the same story over much of the Old West. Bob could see and even smell and hear how the empty land was filling up with new construction, people, noise, traffic, and pollution. Housing developments were built right next to his Phoenix ranch, so close that Bob could have waved to his new neighbors. The ranch was already hemmed in by the canal on the north and a road on the south; the road, which so few cars once had traveled that rabbits hopped across at their leisure, now thundered with traffic. But as time went by, new construction blocked both the other ranch boundaries. This squeezing of the property served also to emphasize Amy's growth and size. Bob's world, and not just the trailer, was getting too small for her. She had outgrown her stall, her paddock, the barn gallery, her trailer, and the ranch itself.

One evening at a dinner party in Scottsdale, Bob was sitting next to a woman visitor from St. Louis. He took out his billfold as usual and showed her photographs of Amy, and told her how he had come to adopt her. He rhapsodized about their lives together, and the woman, an animal lover who raised horses, was enthralled. In passing, Bob mentioned his concerns over how big Amy was growing.

"Why don't you let me find her a home at the St. Louis

Zoo?" the woman asked him; as a member of the zoo's board of directors she could have arranged the adoption with a single telephone call.

"No," Bob said, and thanked her politely. But before leaving the party that night, he went up to her and said, "I may be in touch," and they exchanged business cards.

On the way home he brooded over what he had said to the woman; he felt as if he had betrayed Amy with his words.

"What's the matter, Bob?" Jane asked.

"Nothing," he told her. But it wasn't nothing. It was one of the biggest decisions he would ever have to make.

A subtle change in Bob began after that night. It took the form of a gradual withdrawal, a slight avoidance, and emotional separation. He was being left behind, again—he, the Marlboro Man and a lifelong cowboy who was supposed to be forever young. He *had to let go*. Out of the blue he would say things to Amy like, "I sure would miss you."

Amy had almost always given Bob what he had asked; she had learned to lie down and roll up her trunk and blow a harmonica, and even tap the keys on a piano. She had helped him with his work and was his companion on the ranch. She was his friend and he was her "matriarch." Her world revolved around him and the ranch, the road journey between Colorado and Arizona, and the desert ranch in Phoenix. He was as wrapped up in her welfare as he had ever been with his children's. But, he came to see clearly, she was an elephant living in a human's world, and nothing could make her what she wasn't. Nothing could ever transform her into a smaller, more compact animal. The horse trailer and a barn and paddock were for farm animals, not an elephant. She could not be made to disappear at the Arizona border. She was big. She was an elephant.

In a way she was ready to take on a wider world of humans than Bob had raised her in. She had to move on, and he had to let her go. He had known this for some time, but he had always chosen to wait, to delay, and to pretend. Just as a unique coincidence had brought Bob and Amy together from far apart, another unique circumstance was separating them now. Amy was no steer, no dog, cat, or horse. She was intelligent, with a distinct character and personality. She was trained. She needed more than he could give her. Bob had been blind to everything about her except his feelings, but now circumstances were forcing him to see.

One day, like a tailor fitting a large woman for a ball gown, he took her measurements from trunk to tail, feet to forehead, and all around her stomach. She *was* big, there was no denying it. Sadly he measured her one more time, stooping under and leaning around and over her, then marking each measurement on a sheet of paper. When he made his calculations, the tape told him that she had outgrown his world altogether.

He sat down at his desk and, out of a sense of desperation, drew a design for a transporter that would be big enough to accommodate her. He sketched a customized vehicle with a Plexiglas bubble top for Amy to see out of, heaters and vents, a hay bin, and companion compartments for Michelle and Butch. When he was finished with the drawing, he asked a mechanic who specialized in custom auto work whether the design was feasible.

The man looked at Bob's drawings. "Sure, I can build it," he said. "The problem is whether the law will let you take it out on the road."

"Don't circuses haul elephants?"

"I don't know about that," the man told him. "I assume so. They use railroad train cars and big semi trucks, not a trailer you'll pull behind your truck, Bob."

The man from the USDA arrived at the ranch again. Bob was polite, but he had a feeling about what he was going to say.

He was the same inspector as before, wearing the same rubber boots and green jumpsuit and apparently carrying the same clipboard. With Bob's permission, he looked around again; he didn't need to measure Amy. He was far more interested in the dimensions of the places where she lived, and whether Bob had made the required changes. The regulations, he announced, had been changed; now the USDA was making more stringent demands. Principal among them were requirements for strengthened fences in her paddock, new gates, and a whole new barn for her to live in, designed according to the government agency's specifications. The inspector took all day taking new measurements.

"She's still too big for that stall, even though I see you've widened it," he told Bob. "You'll have to break out that wall again or build a new barn for her from scratch." He paused. "There's also the issue of the ceiling. Your elephant can still conceivably reach her trunk into the electric conduits. Those will either have to be moved, or else you'll have to raise the roof." He enumerated again the list of mandatory changes. He slipped his clipboard under his arm. "I'll be back," he promised for the second time.

Bob watched him leave, beginning to hurt inside with the thought of what he must do about Amy. Throughout his youth he had wondered about this gift of his: He had made himself into a cowboy to be with animals. And now, yet again, as it had been long ago with Lulu, he was finding to his deep regret that his empathy with animals carried with it the greater pain of separation.

Not just anybody could take care of Amy. She would not obey the ranch hands who baby-sat when Bob went away. Bob and Jane could not leave T Cross for even a weekend together, because of her. Amy accepted only Bob as her caretaker and friend, and Jane was getting truly fed up with the restrictions her needs had placed on their lives.

Their own children had grown up and left. These years

should have been their time to enjoy themselves alone, after all the parenting. But with Amy to care for, they were perennial parents of a child that would never leave them.

Jane confided to a friend, "Bob is like an alcoholic with her. It's like he's saying, 'I got to face reality here. I got to stop this.' He realizes that she is too big to handle and it's time to move on, but what can he do about it? He can't go *anywhere*. He knows how nailed down he is. Amy is like having a new baby that never gets older. Bob is in full charge of her, and there's just no time for us to do anything else."

The crisis only worsened one night when Jane was flipping channels and stopped at the sight of an amateur video on one of the shock TV shows, recording the horror experienced by a keeper at the San Diego Zoo. He appeared to hit an elephant in his care, named Cindy. He struck her with the hook end of an *ankus*. Suddenly reacting to the abuse, Cindy snatched the hook out of his hands. She trumpeted with rage, picked the man up, and threw him high in the air over a tall steel fence.

As Jane watched she could not help but ask herself, *Could this ever be Amy?*

The video left a startled impression on her that did not soon go away. She told Bob about the TV. He was unfazed. "I trust Amy," he said. "She would *never* do such a thing."

"But she might hurt you and not mean to."

"Just like horses," he said.

Jane shook her head. "You can get around a horse. You can't get around her. Amy is huge."

He smiled. His smiles always worked with Jane. "She's still my little girl." Jane did not soften.

"Oh, Bob, you refuse to see her as she is. You love her and have no fear of her. How much longer can you go on?" Jane thought again about the video on TV: The zoo attendant had been working with the elephant just as Bob worked in Amy's stall. "Bob, you work around her and bend over and pick up things that she drops. You never look up to see what she's doing; that's dangerous."

"He hit the elephant, you said?"

"Yes."

"I'd never do that to Amy. Never have."

She just looked at him, frustrated by his resolve.

Maybe some part of what she said was true, Bob thought. He did not worry for himself. But he *was* responsible. It was just like Lulu. He asked himself what his father had probably asked about Lulu at the time, "What if she injures somebody? I *am* responsible."

Jane worried as well about their legal liability and what they risked losing if Amy injured someone and they were sued. She told Bob, "Think about it. In a single stroke everything we've worked for could be taken away from us. *What are those years worth*?"

The next day Bob called his lawyer for a legal opinion. "Should I let her continue to do her little act at the schools for the kids?"

"No!" replied the lawyer. "Emphatically no! And in my opinion you never should have let her from the start."

One afternoon, feeding Amy in her stall, Bob asked his son Bobby, who was home visiting, to lend a hand.

Bob was in Amy's stall. "Come on in, it's okay," he told Bobby.

Bobby straddled Amy's rubber food tub. Amy pushed him against the wall with her forehead.

"Dad? She's pushin' into me."

"Hard?"

"Hard now."

Bob said, "Amy, no no."

Bob wondered, What if he had not been there to tell her no? Would she have hurt Bobby?

He thought, She's still young by elephant standards. She'll outlive me, that's for sure. So what will become of her if anything happens to me and she's still here? Who will decide for her? Eventually there will have to be a change. Amy is young enough right now to adjust to another environment. It's the right time; she's in good shape. She has recovered from what ailed her from over in the jungle; she enjoys life. She is disciplined. She wouldn't hurt me, but what if she hurts someone else when I'm not looking? What happens to her then? Does someone shoot her? Is that fair?

T. J. was walking through the gallery. Bob stopped him and began talking about where *he* thought Amy should go. He prefaced the discussion. "No matter what is decided, *if* I decide, if it doesn't work, we can always get her back. We could go and get her and bring her home. Couldn't we?"

"I guess so," said T. J. who felt only a sense of relief. All the ranch hands knew that Amy was too big for Bob to handle anymore.

"What kind of place do you think would suit her? I mean, what people do you think would she be the most comfortable with?"

"Well," said T. J. "Amy is smart."

"She can't go just anywhere."

"What if she was returned to the jungle?"

"She's too domesticated for that," Bob replied. "Besides, they're shooting the elephants over there. Am I going to send her somewhere to be shot?"

"What about zoos?"

Bob recalled his conversation with the woman from St. Louis. "That might be worth looking into."

"Circuses?"

"It'd keep her mind busy. She wouldn't get bored."

"Well?"

Bob sighed. "I just don't know."

Bob felt woefully uninformed, and he wanted to know every option for Amy before he began to make an informed decision. He read that 625 elephants lived in captivity in the United States, 349 of them located in one hundred zoos and safari parks. Zoos, in spite of his misgivings about them, must be doing something right.

He also became familiar with the writings of an eminent British zoologist named Sylvia Sykes, and her definitive work on elephants, *The Natural History of the African Elephant* in which she wrote that captive elephants "respond to serious training with intelligence, obedience and apparent enjoyment, just as they respond to the dignity and pomp of royal ceremony." According to Sykes, elephants working in circuses were healthier mentally and physically than those in zoos. "To some extent, winter work with a circus may replace the need and fulfill the urge of captive elephants to migrate annually."

In the days that followed, Bob went to visit the nearby Phoenix Zoo. What he saw interested him. The zoo had two elephants at that time. One, an Asian named Ruby, drew "pictures" with paint and was a local celebrity popular with children.

Bob felt hopeful, thinking he might have found just the right solution. He reasoned, if Amy went to live at this zoo, she would be cared for day and night by professional elephant handlers. Best of all, he lived half the year no more than fifteen miles away. She would have a "paddock," and though she would not be allowed to wander around as freely as she did at the ranch, she could entertain children visitors to the zoo with her "act" to keep her mind sharp. Bob wrote his proposal to the zoo's directors, offering Amy to them as a gift, with the proviso that he and Amy be allowed to perform a couple of times a week for kids.

"We are a *zoo*, not a circus," the zoo explained to him in a reply.

Bob called them up to argue his case. "What about the elephant that draws the pictures?" he wanted to know. "Isn't she entertainment?"

"That's different."

"How so?"

"It is an elephant doing what it likes to do with paint on a sheet of paper."

"Amy likes to do her act."

"Sorry," he was told. "It just won't work for us."

Bob didn't give up on zoos. He dismissed the disappointment with the Phoenix Zoo as a misunderstanding. And in the weeks that followed, he flew to San Diego to visit its famous zoo. He dined with one of that zoo's directors and asked all the right questions. What bothered Bob more than anything about zoos in general was that he saw the animals just standing around as if they were bored. He returned one last time to the San Diego Zoo. In every season, no matter when he looked in on them, the zoo's elephants still seemed bored. He owed Amy at least the basic freedom to use her brain. She was educated. He had taught her discipline and, to some extent, responsibility. Turning his back on that, he thought, was tantamount to cruelty. One after another he went down a list of zoos: Topiaries, he thought, because that was what the zoo elephants had looked like to him. Amy was no shrub.

Bob trusted Army Maguire more than anyone else on the

subject of elephants. He knew elephants, and he knew Amy. Bob called him and explained his problem. It was a call that did not surprise Maguire. He had learned at their first meeting how unprepared Bob was for Amy's future. He knew how Amy would grow, and how her world would shrink until something had to be done.

Bob asked him, "What choices do I have?"

Maguire replied without hesitation, "Let me answer you this way: You don't."

Bob laughed nervously. "That's helpful."

"You have to make a decision about her. She's too big for you to handle, and she's getting bigger every day. Right?"

"Right," said Bob.

"And you want her to go somewhere that's as good as your place."

"Exactly," said Bob.

"You want to entrust her to the very best. You want to know the people who will care for her."

"That's right, if I can," said Bob. "I'm not going to let her go to perfect strangers. It's why I'm calling you, Army."

"You ruled out zoos."

"She'd be bored."

"What does that leave you with?"

"You tell me."

Maguire thought a moment. "It leaves you with this: two friends of mine who know elephants better than anyone else. If they are interested, they could provide Amy with a home that you would accept. They're great people. They're elephant people."

"I told you," said Bob. "I don't want her going to live with strangers."

"What do you need to know?"

"What more can you tell me? Make them not strangers to me, and then we'll see where we go from there."

"He's *called* Buckles," Maguire said. "It's his circus nickname. Remember this. He's the greatest elephant man alive. Putting you and Amy together with him is like putting a cap on a whiskey bottle. It *belongs*."

CHAPTER SEVEN

William Woodcock had earned his nickname, "Buckles," after he was caught running away *from* the circus as a boy, and his father tied him to a tent pole with looped-together leather belts. Buckles hated the big-top life of his father, a renowned elephant trainer. Elephants didn't appeal to Buckles either. The first time he went to see a circus, at the age of six, the pachyderms left no lasting impression. He took home only memories of the sideshow entertainer who had stuffed his mouth with billiard balls and a live white mouse, which peeked out of his puckered lips.

Buckles worked for his father, which meant that he eventually joined the circus, liking it or not. In the years of the Great Depression, there were few other jobs to choose from. He learned his limitations as a trainer early on. Elephants regularly knocked him down and rolled him around in the gravel. Once one of them walked on him, with her foot on his chest. He was taken straight to a hospital.

Buckles told the doctor, "I'm a little sore."

The doctor said, "What happened to you?"

"An elephant stepped on me."

"Of course you are."

Buckles's wife, Barbara, also came from a circus family. Her mother trained elephants to water-ski. Her family owned the Greene Wild Animal Farm in Vermont, which featured a llama act and two mean zebras. Her father owned the eponymous Ray's Night at the Circus and Ray Bros. Circus. From an early age she had wanted to work with elephants. But she fell in love instead with an elephant man named Rex. Engaged to be married to him at thirteen, she was married at fourteen and a mother at sixteen. Rex soon revealed himself to be a rascal. One evening, dinner was on the table, Barbara was waiting for him to return from the store a block away with a loaf of bread. Three days later Rex came back. After eleven stormy years of marriage, Rex had used up all his excuses, and Barbara divorced him to begin, finally, to train *elephants*, having failed with an elephant *man*.

Barbara in those days was a stunning-looking woman, with long red hair, a fine athletic figure, a flair for the circus, and a strong will. She had admirers from Havana to New York City, of whom one was Buckles. Tall, dark, and brooding, he wore colored silk turbans and military jackets, with brass buttons and gold-fringed epaulets. She was small and seemed as light as air in her gossamer veils, sequined pants, and halter.

They started their married life in 1959 with a "fleabag outfit" that called itself the Tom Mix Circus. The owner's wife was nicknamed "Catfish" Claire, and his mother was called "Mud." He changed its name to Bernum[sic] Brothers and put up pictures of P. T. Barnum, calling the founder of the Barnum & Bailey Circus "Our Founder." From there the newly married Woodcocks went out on their own with elephants named Anna May and Lydia. They opened in the dead of winter, offering elephant rides for a quarter apiece. When they scraped together a couple of dollars, they said, "There's a bale of hay for Anna May." The next couple of dollars went for hay for Lydia, and so on. Once Barbara and Buckles shared a half loaf of bread for three days.

Barbara put them on the circus map when she dressed up their act and glamorized it with her presence. Suddenly they were a young couple in demand, featured with three trained elephants, a lovely wardrobe, and a top-notch act. They signed with a big-time promoter who ran off with their money. But they got lucky when Ed Sullivan chose them to perform on his TV show in 1965, and then asked them back four more times.

Buckles had earned a reputation as a fine elephant trainer. Over the years he worked with a generation of elephant men and founded Ringling's celebrated elephant breeding/research farm in Florida. Kenneth Feld, the owner of Ringling Bros. and Barnum & Bailey Circus, had such respect for

Buckles that he called him to rescue Ringling's elephants when the circus's Blue Train flew off the rails in early 1991.

The train was fifty-three cars long and carried 150 performers, twenty-three elephants, and about one hundred other animals, including lions, tigers, bears, and horses. It was rolling through Lakeland, Florida, early one morning, when a grinding scream of metal echoed through the cars. The train derailed, flinging sixteen middle cars off the tracks. Dazed midgets, Russian acrobats, animal handlers, and clowns stumbled out of the wreck.

Rescuers found the lifeless body of Ringling's elephant man, a Buckles protégé. He had been sitting on a wooden box in a baggage car with his stepsons on either side of him. At the instant of the crash, a refrigerator flew down the length of the car and crushed him to death. Now there was no one to take charge of the elephants trapped in the front of the train. Nervous and upset, trumpeting and harrumphing, they waited to be rescued.

Buckles had heard the news as he was about to leave the house on the Woodcock's farm in Ruskin, Florida. The phone rang. Feld was calling to ask him to please lend a hand. Buckles had nothing to do with Ringling at the time, but he was out the door in minutes.

Buckles knew the preferences, moods, emotions, and, he believed, the minds of Asian elephants. In contrast, Africans were complete strangers to him. Most elephant people did not give Africans credit for personality and character. What little Buckles knew about them was colored by myth and prejudice. It was true that his father had compared them to pterodactyls, claiming that "all their brains are in their ears." Never actually having seen or worked with one in person, he had believed it.

Buckles's favorite elephant was the old Asian, Anna May. She was gentle and accepting, a sweet, nurturing matriarch who had started her career in show business at the same time as the Woodcocks. Barbara felt even stronger emotions toward Anna May. Indeed, she was a heroine to her. In the middle of a performance in Houston one evening the stage floor had collapsed under Anna May's weight, and both Anna May and Barbara had fallen. Barbara's head smashed against a pedestal, but Anna May stopped her from falling through the floor and thus probably saved her life. Anna May stayed calm even though she was bleeding heavily from a deep gash in her leg. She carried Barbara to Buckles and laid her across his arms.

When she returned after several days in the hospital with a bandaged head, Barbara went first thing to visit Anna May. As she went past them, the other elephants reached out to her with their trunks, begging for goodies, but not Anna May. She stretched her trunk, Barbara remembers, to touch her bandage tenderly, and, Barbara says, she breathed an elephant's sigh of relief.

As a classic one-ring circus under a big-top tent, the Big Apple Circus was an ideal place for an act like the Woodcocks and their elephants to perform. The Big Apple

enjoyed a virtuous reputation: It valued its animal performers and showed them with an appealing simplicity. All by
themselves—without gymnastics, fancy costumes, and elaborate routines—the elephants made children laugh. The Big
Apple toured like any circus but only in New York State,
New England, Chicago, and Atlanta, and its leisurely schedule was easy on its human and animal performers alike.

Once a day, and sometimes twice on matinee days, Buckles and his elephants performed under the big top. The elephants amazed the audiences with their size and often
inspired in them feelings of awe. *What great, mighty beasts these
really are!* their expressions seemed to say. The elephants
moved swiftly on silent feet, with only the whisper of their
breath to mark their passing around the ring in a rhythm of
bulk and grace. Under the colored lights they appeared to
be almost weightless, changing before children's eyes into
magical and improbable beasts invented in dreams.

One afternoon while Buckles was relaxing in the Woodcocks' Freightliner RV, parked alongside the elephant enclosure at Lincoln Center in New York City, Army Maguire
called to say hello, as he did now and then just to keep in
touch. Maguire, among Buckles's many other friends, kept
him current on the elephant world's gossip.

Maguire said, "I know a guy that's got an African elephant. It's getting too big for him to handle. He's looking
into zoos."

"That's a shame," Buckles replied. "You don't want a trained elephant walking around like a lump in a zoo."

"I told him all about you and Barbara, and that you would take good care of her. I told him you'd keep her working and her mind sharp."

"Hold on a minute, Army. You're getting ahead of me. As far as I'm concerned, taking on an African elephant is like getting married."

"What's that, Buckles?"

Buckles laughed. "Like a wife, they give more than they want, and less than you'd like."

"So?"

"I'm already married."

"Listen to me," said Maguire. "I'm telling you, this elephant is special. It's not the tricks she does. It's *her*, it's her *personality*."

"She's still an African."

"And she deserves a good home. I'm asking you to think about it."

By chance, a recent change left room for a new elephant in his troop. One of his elephants was an Asian named Peggy. She saw ghosts and frightened Buckles as no elephant had ever done before. She needed constant watching; she was dangerous, unpredictable, and even violent. She hated some people on sight and lashed out at them with her trunk. Buckles never knew what she was thinking or what she might do, and he worried incessantly. What if she started seeing ghosts again like she did in Staten Island. . . ?

Buckles related the story on the phone. "The only time an elephant ever scared the hell out of me was when we were down there. I was looking at Peggy. She was kind of barking, like a dog. She'd look off in an oblique direction. She wouldn't stop eating or drinking either. She'd be rocking on her legs. She'd constantly look in that same direction. That night we had a show. She wasn't responding to anything. Regardless what I did to her, she turned back to look in that same direction. We were going in to do the act. Anna May and Peggy were 'tailed-up,' and Peggy whipped around, and then she was beside Anna May walking backward, with Anna May's tail in her trunk. She was looking in that same direction as before, at the ghosts. We entered like always. Anna May came in line and Peggy came in line that way, still looking back. She was rocking. So then we went around the ring in the opening trick. They brought in the lion. Anna May saluted. Peggy turns the wrong way and was looking through the band in that same direction. I pulled her around. I hollered at Anna May. And Anna May was holding onto Peggy, and Peggy was shaking like a leaf. I took them out right away."

Buckles wondered, What if something happens to me and I am laid up and can't take care of her? No one else can even get near her.

It was time, Buckles felt certain, to retire Peggy to an Asian elephant sanctuary that he knew about in Tennessee.

The show could go on without her, but there would be an empty place in the act to fill.

"I'll have Barbara call him," Buckles told Maguire, who had already given him Bob's name and telephone number. "I'm not telling you I will or I won't. Let's see first what he has to say."

After enough time went past, Bob had forgotten the conversation with Maguire, when a woman called. She said her name was Barbara Woodcock, and she sounded friendly and homespun.

"I know just what you're going through."

"You *do*?"

"My, yes. My husband and I have had only one vacation in thirty-nine years of marriage." She sounded as if she didn't mind in the least.

"That's part of it," said Bob. "It's a *big* part of it."

"You devote your life to them. You have to. Elephants spoil you for people. Am I right?"

"Well, yes—"

"We don't mind—my husband, Buckles, and me. Elephants are like people to us. That's what they are."

"Would you like to meet her—meet Amy?" Bob asked.

She paused ominously. "I just don't know the answer to that," she said.

"But you are calling about Amy?"

"Army told us she is a beautiful animal. He said that you and she have a wonderful relationship."

"I love her, that's true," said Bob.

"Army said she's very special. Maybe we *should* meet her." She paused and lowered her voice. "But I'm going to have a tough time convincing my husband. He's set his mind against Africans. His father did too. He said their brains were all in their ears. He didn't like them in the least."

"He'll like Amy," said Bob. "I'll bet on it."

Bob was convinced that he was doing what was right. The choice of Buckles should have been almost easy. But it wasn't. Saying good-bye to Amy, he knew, was going to be the hardest thing he ever had to do.

CHAPTER EIGHT

B

ob glanced at the blue sky, and, with the thought of what he had to do, tears welled up in his eyes. Standing halfway between his truck and the horse barn, ready to enter Amy's stall and as ready to climb back in the truck and drive away, he thought, If only I hadn't let her mean so much to me.

In his lifetime he had said good-bye to horses, dogs, and Lulu the bear. He had said tearful farewells to his grandfather Angell, his mom and dad, and his brothers. Yet none of those was more painful than now. He sighed as he looked off toward the foothills and peaks of the Rockies, knowing that something profound and special had touched his life. He had given his heart to an elephant. He managed a smile at that thought, and wiped his eyes as he turned into the barn.

He stopped before the Dutch doors of her stall to try out

a smile he did not feel but that he hoped would deceive her. It was useless: Smiles, no smiles, or tears, he believed that she always knew what his heart felt.

He leaned his shoulder almost casually against the door-frame. He recalled the day they first met, in this stall, back when she was an orphaned baby, too scared to put her trunk over the door. He looked in, and when she saw him she walked over to greet him. Michelle bleated and stood beside her; Michelle came up to Amy's knee now. He took off his cowboy hat and held it in both hands in front of him-self. He smoothed back his hair. He opened his mouth, but words failed him. He cleared his throat. He wished he had a drink of water. Trying hard not to cry, he wiped his cheeks on his sleeve.

"I'm sorry . . ."

He had promised himself not to get emotional in front of her, and now this!

"We got to let you go, Amy," he said in a soft voice. "I don't want you to worry. We can always get you back if you don't like it, or if it ever goes wrong for you, I promise you that." He worked up a thin smile. "You'll like the place where you're going. I guarantee it's going to be fun. There are other elephants there to play with. Yes, sir, you're going to New York City where there's the finest plays and operas." He choked up. "This is a sad day, and I'm melancholy about it. I'm going to miss you, sweetheart."

Amy curled the end of her trunk around Bob's wrist and drew his hand in to her. As she did in quiet times when they were together, when she needed his reassurance, she placed his hand in her mouth to let him pet her there. She seemed to sense his emotions in deeper ways. Bob thought that she knew what was happening, and he believed that she trusted him to decide for her what was right. For any animal, change evoked ancient fears of the unknown: starvation, thirst, and even death. Amy would have to be brave. She was losing the compass of her life, as Bob saw himself, and she might not know what to do or even how to feel. He was her "matriarch," her family, her herd. Her knowledge and understanding of the human world, like her sustenance and health, had largely flowed from him. Her life included him completely; he had given her time and patience and a safe environment. Now strong and healthy, she probably could not imagine a life without him in it.

Bob thought, I am lucky. He had crossed the divide of animal and human understanding. He knew how "animal people" stood apart. Animals had shaped his whole life as a cowboy, and out of nowhere a hurt animal had come to him—what difference *what* she was? Amy had needed his help. Now his heart felt as if it was breaking.

It was a crowded trailer with Amy, Michelle, Butch, and a horse named Zorro, along with Amy's electric piano and her green ball and toys. The tires sagged as Bob put the truck in gear and slowly started out for the last time. They bumped on the gravel drive past the ranch hands looking sad to see Amy go. They waved their hats and yelled good-bye. T. J.

tried to smile, but he knew he was losing a friend. By the edge of the wallow Bob craned his neck out of the truck cab. He called back to Amy, "Wave bye-bye, sweetheart, wave bye-bye!"

They drove south and east to Bobby's Texas horse ranch, where Bob was turning Amy over to Buckles, who was then to take her east to his farm in Florida. She was going to stay there until she was ready to join the Big Apple Circus, and that could take time. She was going to need to get used to the Woodcocks and their elephants, Anna May and Ned. But mostly she was going to have to get used to life without Bob.

On the road Bob stared at the yellow stripes that flicked hypnotically past. The horn blasts of passing trucks, the waves of children in passing cars, the shifting of her weight, and the sounds of her playing her piano no longer had the same meanings as before. He had a terrible job to do.

There was no *good* way of telling her good-bye. He thought, Good-byes are like little deaths. He had never felt as close to humans as to some of the animals in his life. Amy had stolen his heart. Now he pretended that this good-bye was the start of a better life. She might not even miss him. She had Michelle and her favorite green ball and her other toys, "monkey" biscuits, and a bag of El Chorro's sticky buns.

Too soon, it seemed, he was driving into his son Bobby's ranch. Amy got out of the trailer and stretched her legs, drank, and ate, while Bob greeted Buckles. They talked about the road conditions and the weather, and this and that. Bob was thinking of the inevitable. Distractedly, he told Buckles, "She likes carrots in the morning and buns, and if you can get them where you are in Florida, she likes strawberries dipped in chocolate."

He walked over to Amy. He petted her trunk and whispered to her, "Good-bye."

He told Buckles. "I can't stay any longer. I got to go." He walked away and did not look back. As he drove out of the ranch gates, he thought, I lost two brothers, and now this hurts almost as bad.

CHAPTER NINE

At the end of the journey to Florida, Amy looked around, trying to find Bob. Michelle followed her out of the trailer. Amy searched for a single familiar sight. She hugged Michelle around her middle, two orphans, staring out at their new world.

Buckles tried to reassure Amy. He called to her to follow him around the drive to a tall gate that opened onto a green pasture unlike any other that Amy had ever seen. This one was overgrown with tall grass and with palmettos growing wild. Amy looked at the food that was offered, but it wasn't what she was used to. She walked over to a water trough, like the one she had dipped her trunk in when she was a baby in Africa. The water tasted warm, with none of the freshness of the ranch. Dark clouds filled the sky, and from far off came the rumble of thunder. Rain threatened to pour.

She knew the old route at the ranch, from her stall into her paddock, where her toys were kept, and from there into the pasture, to her wallow, or along the drive that formed a circle in front of the horse barn. She probably could have walked on her own along the ranch fences or up to the water tank, where she sometimes went with Bob. Her old world had been strictly defined. Now she backed up into the corner of the Woodcocks' pasture and looked out, clearly confused and frightened by the newness of it all.

Buckles unloaded her toys in the barn, where Ned and Anna May were standing in their stalls. He patted Anna May on the nose, then went to put food in Amy's new stall and open the doors for her to come in when she wanted to. Barbara joined him there as he was loosening a hay bale. She was anxious to see the newest family member. From across the pasture she saw Amy, and Barbara's heart went out to her.

"I don't care if you're a gopher—when your world changes, there's an adjustment to be made, and Amy has to do it," Buckles explained, seeing the look on Barbara's face. "Her world has changed, and she doesn't know what's going on. It's just something she'll have to get through. She'll have to do it herself."

"What about Anna May?" asked Barbara.

He knew what she was asking; Anna May was the matriarch. "I'll put Amy out with her once she's seen her new stall. We'll see if it helps."

That night Amy heard the sounds of other elephants for the first time since her childhood, and smelled their smell. She beat the walls of her stall with her trunk, hugged Michelle, and waited for the morning as if she hoped that Bob would be standing by her stall door with fresh-cut carrots in his hand, just like always.

Instead of carrots, the sight of her own elephant kind greeted her. She had last seen an elephant long enough ago perhaps not to remember. Amy was of the species *Loxodonta africana*, while Ned and Anna May, as Asian elephants, were classified *Elephas maximus*. There were plain differences in their sizes and shapes, the fingers of their trunks, their ears, their teeth, the curvature of their backs, the shape of their heads, and so on. But their similarities, at least in humans' eyes, were greater by far than their differences.

Watching Amy watch Anna May and Ned, Buckles explained to Barbara, "It's like if I was raised in a herd of buffalo and I saw another human," he said. "I'd *know* I was more like the human than the buffalo. I'd be confused and maybe scared. Amy is too. She's seeing for the first time that she isn't a horse and she isn't a human. She is an elephant. That may come as a shock. She'll try to communicate, but whether she succeeds, we may never know."

Even more than anyone imagined, Amy missed Bob. Buckles had no other explanation for her behavior. And she clearly longed to return to the ranch, Buckles believed, as though life itself had been stolen from her. She stood as a ghostly figure in the corner of the Woodcocks' pasture, hour upon hour, staring out at nothing, curious about nothing, not making a sound. She seemed almost to pine, and she only sniffed at her food. Worse still, when Buckles ordered her to move, she refused, as though she were unwilling to take commands from anyone but Bob.

"She won't give me a thing," Buckles told Barbara. "I just don't know what to do with her."

"Just give her time," she replied.

Buckles even started to believe that he had made a bad choice. His father was probably right about African elephants. Buckles had no basis for understanding Amy. He didn't know what to expect. If Amy were Anna May or Ned, he would have known to keep her busy, and she would have soon forgotten all about what depressed her. But how could he keep Amy busy if he could not get her to respond?

He called Bob on the telephone, ostensibly to report that they had successfully made the journey from Texas to Florida. "She misses you," he told Bob.

"That makes two of us."

Buckles told Bob about her odd behavior, and he asked him, "You got any idea how to make her snap out of it?"

"Chocolate-covered strawberries."

"That's it? That's all?"

"That and what your wife, Barbara, says, just give her time to get used to it."

Anna May and Ned left Amy alone.

Ned, a rambunctious bull, was spoiled by Anna May. He had never shared with another elephant his own age, and he clearly wasn't about to now. Even—perhaps especially—in Amy's presence, Anna May treated Ned as her own baby. She tickled him and played with him. Ned liked being tickled, and he trumpeted, tossed his head, and went all loose and silly. He also loved to be scared. Buckles contended that the young elephant woke up each morning telling himself, I hope something happens today that I can be afraid of. Wouldn't it be great if I could be afraid? It doesn't have to be anything large. Just real scary. Ned worked harder than any elephant Buckles had ever known to find excuses *not* to do what Buckles asked him to. Every day was a battle of wits, and according to Buckles, Ned woke up each morning with elaborate, fully conceived plans to get out of working. "He must have exhausted himself just thinking them up," he said.

More than anything else, except for food, Ned loved his B. F. Goodrich tire. He rolled the tire at his side and stuffed it with hay for snacks. He hugged it. He slept with it by his side. The circus roustabouts sometimes teased him by hiding the tire under bales of hay. Ned cried and carried on until the tire was returned. Barbara had to tell the circus manager to make the roustabouts stop tormenting him; Ned was obsessed, even for an elephant, with his tire.

Buckles had never witnessed such a withdrawal and depression as Amy's. He despaired for her. As he'd said to Barbara, she was giving him nothing: She wasn't eating; she hardly moved; she looked sick. Anyone could see that she was losing weight. Buckles no longer worried whether Amy would get along with Ned and Anna May. He wondered if she would live. And he pondered whether to just send her back to Bob.

He got on the phone to talk to him about her. And what he learned surprised him. Bob was feeling the same effects of separation as Amy. Since they had said good-bye, he had slipped into a surprising depression, the first in his life of any magnitude. He said little about it to Jane, but he felt all adrift. He rode his horses with no enthusiasm, and he wandered off for long periods of time alone. Sometimes he just stood at Amy's wallow staring at the reflections of the clouds in the muddy water. He still rode the fences, but he rode without the company of the dogs.

One afternoon Jane was looking for him around the house. She called out his name. He had been there minutes ago, and he always told her when he was leaving. She looked through the front window. The horse trailer was parked by the curb. She went to look around the back of the trailer. At the rear gate as she looked in, she saw Bob standing with his back to her, all alone, bent over Amy's little piano. She could tell that he was crying. She turned quietly and tiptoed back to the house. When she later asked him about it, he explained simply, "Hell, she was my girl."

On the telephone now, Bob told Buckles, "I said she could come home if it didn't work out. Maybe she just wants to come home, Buckles. I don't know what to tell you. I just don't know. Did you try the trick with the strawberries?"

"I did," said Buckles, who felt awkward calling Bob—*he* was the elephant man. Yet Amy's depression perplexed him. "Any other ideas?" he asked Bob. "You know her. Maybe you know what might jog her out of it."

"Try a toy," said Bob. "It's all I can suggest. It helped her when she first came here. Maybe it will help her now."

When he hung up, Bob sat down, utterly dejected. He *had* made the right decision to let her go, but he realized that, in a sense, she was not gone; she was in his heart, where she would remain until the day he died.

Ned was busy eating hay when Amy first *saw* his tire. Ned felt confident by this time, nearly six weeks after Amy arrived in Florida, that his tire was safe around her. He apparently no longer felt the urgent need to guard it all day long. Ned looked up from his food bin and let out a terrible elephant scream.

Amy was touching his tire! Now Amy was rolling his tire!

"You'd think somebody was killing him," said Barbara, looking out the window.

"Well, it *is* his good friend," said Buckles.

"Not anymore."

"Ouch!" said Buckles.

Ned had bitten Amy's tail.

In a remarkable way, Ned's tire helped Amy adjust to her new life.

"It was that and more," Barbara reported to Bob. "It's Ned's reaction when she takes the tire. She's egging him on. She knows what she's doing, and she enjoys teasing him. He is such a baby. He plays right into her hands every time."

"She's just smarter than Ned is," Barbara told Bob, whom she called with the news. "I swear to you, she torments him. She has fun at it. She may still miss you, Bob, but she found something to take her mind off it. She's dealing with a dummy. He's an easy one to trick; if you could see him, you'd feel sorry for him."

"I would?" Bob felt like laughing.

"He protects his tire now all the time. He bellows when she comes near it. He can never quite figure out if she's going to try to steal it, and he ends up with hurt feelings.

Buckles scolded Amy the other day, and the scolding pleased Ned. I swear."

Bob felt his depression lighten as he listened to her talk. What she said was funny and strange enough to be true. He had never met Ned, but he could picture him. Amy had teased the colts on the ranch; she was smarter and easily outwitted them. Clearly, he thought, she was doing the same thing with Ned.

"Ned won't let her hold his tail," Barbara was saying. "They're supposed to be doing that at the opening of the act."

"It's a small price to pay," Bob told her.

"That's not all. She waits until he is asleep or he's eating, and she pokes him with her tusks. She lulls him into standing in front of her, then she gives him a good jab in the rump."

"Keep it up!" Bob told her.

Hanging up the phone, he thought, If Amy can get over it, I can too!

Anna May, almost forty years older than Amy and Ned, missed her girlfriend, Peggy, who had retired to the sanctuary in Tennessee. In the years that they were together Peggy and Anna May had often stood side by side in the barn and in the pasture, mumbling and grazing and listening to the wind in the palms. Buckles thought that Anna May felt lonely without Peggy. Even more, he thought that she missed another female to include in her *being*. Female elephants doted endlessly on young males and protected them and taught them lessons for life, but, it seemed to Buckles, they could only *be* with other females. Neither scientists nor researchers were able to point to a reason. But Buckles, after years of living with elephants, made a guess: Female elephants *talked* together, gossiped, and generally cluttered the air with their chatter. He had *felt* the evidence of sound vibrations on his skin and heard their sounds with his ears. He declared, "Anna May and Peggy stopped talking only when their mouths were full!"

One day Buckles heard Anna May call out. Amy faced in her direction. Anna May raised her bulbous old head and fanned the air with her small, tattered, spotted ears, as if she were waiting to hear some uttered sound that would tell her that Amy understood her call.

Anna May persisted, Buckles noticed. Over the weeks, she called out to Amy in strange, haunting sounds. One day, without explanation, Buckles felt the air around Amy and Anna May shake with the pressure of sound. Their ears went out and their heads went up. Almost certainly each was listening to what the other elephant had to "say." And if she talked to Anna May, what an amazing tale Amy had to tell her! Even more, if their communication was real, Amy had found a creature in Anna May to *listen* to, an older, wiser animal to possibly help her make sense of all that had happened.

And with that Anna May became Amy's refuge. Amy pushed up against her side and held her trunk in the fingers of her own. She followed her around the pasture, ate when Anna May ate, and drank when Anna May drank. It seemed that Amy was over the worst.

CHAPTER TEN

At the Big Apple Circus, Amy stepped through a looking glass into a topsy-turvy tented world of gaudy clowns, flying acrobats, and magicians with pigeons up their sleeves. This world of new rhythms and colors came alive with people who were more of just about *everything*. And, wildly different though this new world seemed to anyone looking in, nothing about it seemed incongruous or, to the circus entertainers themselves, even particularly strange.

The Big Apple had the appurtenances of an elephant hotel, *with* conveniences. Every detail of Amy's life was examined, reexamined, and thought over twice. Feeding and watering were just the beginning. The circus managers, with Buckles advising them, looked at ventilation and warmth and space for Amy to move around in. Her nails were trimmed and polished regularly; her body was scrubbed with brushes and curried with combs. She was treated as a circus professional, as an entertainer with a temperament, individuality, and emotions, as a celebrity, and, sometimes, as a star.

Amy thrilled Buckles with her recovery. He wondered what his father had meant about the brains of African elephants' being in their ears. Amy was smart, she was talented, and she was the easiest elephant to get along with that he had ever known. He told Barbara, "Bob made her into a perfect lady."

Her new circus routines came as a snap. What more did she need to learn? With Anna May standing by to give her reassurance, she picked up fast on Buckle's instructions. She was a quick study once she decided to learn. Her circus life started with three-year-old Skye, who wore diapers and did not yet know how to talk. Skye was the Woodcocks' granddaughter, who performed in the circus every afternoon by perching in a basket that Ned carried in his mouth. The act typified the level of the Big Apple's performances. Ned was big and Skye was cute and tiny; the difference was simple and the act was undemanding, yet it pleased the crowd.

But one day Skye refused to perform with Ned, and she did not yet have the words to explain why.

After weeks of indulging her, Barbara finally learned that Skye wanted to perform with Amy. By her thinking, Ned was used goods, dull, and not particularly fun. Amy made her laugh and dogged her around the pathways between the circus caravans and in the tent between shows.

In the end Skye got her way. With only a bit of additional training Amy learned to lift her. She bent her leg at the knee and with a gentleness that surprised Barbara, she could swing Skye up on her back in a fluid, graceful motion that made her look like a seasoned professional. Amy lay down on her side to let Skye off, and as she got up again, "waltzed" and "spun" to the audience's applause.

Training an elephant is a delicate affair," Buckles liked to say. "There is no braver beast and no greater coward. There is no better friend and no worse enemy." Though nothing that Buckles asked Amy to do was different from what she would have done in the wild, except for doing them as part of a regular routine, she gave him fits.

"She's like a cat!" he complained to Barbara one day. "She can't be made to like anyone she doesn't want to like. Her own way is the only way, and she doesn't try to please. She is only and always just herself—"

Barbara cut him off. "So, what you're saying, Buckles, she isn't one to wag her tail?"

In their performances Amy was always slightly off cue: She skipped a half beat behind Ned and Anna May. Buckles decided that she had a secret reason. She had discovered the rewards of keeping an eye on the audience. One time, as Ned and Anna May lay down in the ring, Amy lay down—not by coincidence—Buckles believed, in front of three boys in the front row who were sitting with refreshments in their laps. When Buckles turned his head, Amy quickly slithered her trunk over the knee-high barrier that separated the audience from the performers in the ring. She snatched the bags of popcorn from the surprised boys. Buckles had never seen any elephant work faster or with such clear premeditation. Amy was proving herself to be even smarter than Bob had told him. Buckles scolded her after the act was over, but the audience roared its approval at the time.

Amy actually seemed to smile and bask in the approving screams of the children. With their noise in her ears, all on her own, without prompting from Buckles, she acted silly, spreading her ears and letting her trunk go floppy, just like when she played hide-and-seek with Bob.

Her mind was too quick for the repeated routines of an act that changed only once in a circus season. Once she snatched a woman's pocketbook off an empty seat during a performance. She reached out to frisk the audience for treats while Ned and Anna May performed their dramatic "stands." When Amy lay down in the ring, she blew on people, as if the audience were there for *her* amusement. She once held a trunk of water through several minutes of the performance. Then when Buckles turned his back, she showered the audience with a blast of elephant spray.

One day Buckles lined up Amy, Ned, and Anna May for an inspection outside the tent before they entered the ring to perform. Again he turned away for an instant, and that was long enough for Amy to escape. She walked out of the elephant line, over to a circus guest who was pushing his child in a stroller along a path. Amy smelled the man and the baby and searched their clothing for treats. The child laughed. The man reached up and petted her trunk. Amy reached gently down and snatched an ice cream bar out of the child's hand. A moment later she walked through the gate back to her tent to "retire" for the rest of the day.

Buckles was flabbergasted.

"It's all Bob," he told Barbara soon after the incident. "She thinks she's a queen because that was how he treated her."

"But you can't allow her to just wander off," Barbara said.

"I can't? What choice do I have? She has her own mind, and nothing will change it. That's how she is; that's how Bob raised her."

As if to confirm that fact, that same afternoon during rehearsals, when Buckles was working with Ned and Anna May and Amy was supposed to be standing in a corner by herself, she searched around her feet for tidbits of popcorn and candy. Finally, bored with herself, she set off skipping around the ring, first on one front foot, then the other. Buckles and the other performers stopped what they were doing and just stared, as if to say, *There she goes again*!

Buckles again called Bob to report to him the changes that he had seen. "She has all the things we look for in an elephant," he told him. "She's like a thoroughbred racehorse, but she marches to a different drummer."

"I'm glad to hear it," said Bob.

"What, that she's like a racehorse or she marches to a different drummer?"

"Both," said Bob proudly. "I could have told you, Buckles, that if you expected Amy to be right on the dime you'd be disappointed."

"She is unflappable. I'll say that much for her. But she just doesn't seem to know she's in showbiz."

"She always just did things on her own. You have to let her be. She just figures she'd rather do something different sometimes. You can't blame her, either."

She had performed with the Big Apple Circus less than a year before Buckles awarded her a starring role. The act was billed as "The Magic Carpet" and featured Amy and the Big Apple's top clown, Bello Nock, whose "signature" was a shocking palisade of yellow hair. Bello clowned continuously in and out of the ring and quickly recognized Amy as a kindred spirit.

He told Buckles one day, "I mean, she is clownish all by herself without makeup and costumes and an act."

"You mean she likes to get away with murder."

That was partly it. "She likes to see what she can get away with, it's true, but that's what we clowns *do*. She likes to get the better of you, like you were her father. That's why the kids laugh with her. She is always trying to get away with something, like they do at home. She does simple funny things that she isn't asked to do. A*nd* she has good ideas."

As part of "The Magic Carpet," Amy routinely dragged

Bello out of the ring on the "magic" carpet at the finale. She was soon bored with this routine, though, and, Buckles was convinced, was looking for mischief. One day at the end of the performance, she seemed to notice a large pile of elephant dung that Ned had deposited on his way out moments before. Now Amy was pulling Bello on the carpet as usual, when at the last instant, as she was leaving the ring, she swerved off-line and dragged him *through* the manure. The audience screamed louder than Bello had ever heard them. Amy stopped outside the tent and looked at Bello, and he could have sworn that she was smiling.

In feigned anger, he grabbed her trunk in both his hands, speaking sternly into its end as if it were a telephone, then smacking it over his ear, as if he were listening to her reply. "You did that on purpose," he told her. He fanned the seat of his dirty pants, and he thought he saw her mouth curve upward.

With every indication that he thought his hair actually looked handsome, Bello sometimes was seen turning away to primp his pompadour. Amy apparently decided that she could make fun of this vanity. In their act together, Bello pretended to be a waiter in a restaurant. Amy sat on a chair at a table and "read" a menu, while Bello stood by waiting to take her order. Bello walked away, then returned with bread on a tray and was looking at the audience when Amy snatched the bread away. Bello feigned not knowing where the bread had disappeared to. The kids screamed at him: "Amy!"

In the meantime Amy had sucked up a trunkful of water out of a wooden bucket that was placed on the table. And as Bello scolded her for stealing the bread, she sprayed him all over with water. His proud blond cascade of hair wilted and fell in his eyes. The audience screamed its approval. Again Bello was convinced that Amy's mouth curved upward in an elephant's smile.

Slowly, over the months, Amy, Ned, and Anna May formed a family, with Anna May as their unquestioned leader. Amy and Ned were too different in temperament and character ever to get along. Anna May disciplined them both. She knocked them with her trunk and seized their ears with sharp, painful twists. Clearly at the limit of her patience, Anna May lowered her head, butted them, and nipped their tails.

Buckles scolded them. "Aren't you ashamed of yourself, Amy!" he told her when she misbehaved. "A big girl like you and you don't have any more sense than Ned! Well, what have you got to say for yourself?" Amy raised her trunk as if she were pleading with him until Buckles changed his tone. "Well, do you think you can be good now?" She bobbed her head in the affirmative.

On a hot, humid September afternoon during a stop in upstate New York, Amy and Anna May and Ned were being tormented by swarms of flies. Without enough dust and dirt on the ground to shoo them with, the elephants looked miserable. There was nothing Buckles could do. He was resting in his trailer when he heard a loud bellowing noise, and he looked out the window onto a very strange sight.

Amy had found an empty gunnysack lying on the ground. She was swatting the flies off her back with it. She tossed the sack on her right side and the flies took off in a cloud, and then she tossed it on her left side and another cloud departed. She seemed delighted and draped the sack over her ear for future use.

Seeing this, Anna May and Ned wanted to swat the flies too. As Buckles watched, Ned snatched the sack off Amy's ear. Amy whacked Ned with her trunk; he bellowed and dropped the sack. Anna May picked it up and started swatting herself. Now Amy was bellowing, Ned was bellowing, and Anna May was trumpeting with relief. She slung the sack against her sides and back while Ned and Amy waited for their turns.

Buckles decided to intervene before they started fighting all over again. He went to a storage barn on the grounds for two more gunnysacks, which he gave to Ned and Anna May. And from then on Anna May, Amy, and Ned swatted the flies with their own sacks, which they also hung over their ears like garlands.

During that same stop, a prowler was thought to be stealing the personal belongings of the performers through the open windows of their trailers. An investigation was mounted and failed to find either the missing items or a culprit. Then one evening Buckles remembered something his father had told him. Sometimes small objects appealed to elephants, and their playfulness often included theft. So on a hunch Buckles searched their barn. There, concealed under a layer of straw, was the missing loot: a silver-backed brush, change purses, a fringed bedcover, two mirrors, a few photographs in small frames, a beaten-up hat, a shoe, and several pencils!

Buckles scolded Amy, Ned, and Anna May, but he knew that he was in charge of highly intelligent creatures with a sense of mischief that was as much a part of them as their ears, trunks, and tails.

He certainly couldn't do anything to dissuade Ned from smashing soft-drink cans with his foot. For a while flattening them was Ned's whole raison d'être. Then one day he came across an empty gallon can that had been thrown out of the cookhouse door. He licked the residue of sauce from around the inside of the can with the end of his trunk. Then the sudden urge to smash it overpowered him, and he stomped down hard with his foot. The can collapsed with his trunk still inside. He bellowed, screamed out in pain, and tossed his trunk to throw the can off. Buckles came running to his rescue, and Ned walked away grumbling to himself, nursing his sore trunk.

Meanwhile Amy liked to keep a vigil at a hole in the baseboard of the elephant barn. Apparently, she had seen a rat come out of the hole and had flattened the rodent with her trunk. She waited patiently for other rats to emerge, and even slid down on her stomach and poised her trunk over the hole, waiting.

"No cat was more faithful," said Buckles, who felt sorry for her, with all that waiting and nothing to show for it. As a gesture of kindness he wrapped a furry piece of gray cloth with strong rubber bands and poked the "rat" through the hole from the other side of the barn wall. Amy slammed it again and again. She chirruped and trumpeted each time unaware (or unconcerned) that the "rat" she "killed" ten or fifteen times a day was fake.

Other Big Apple animals, such as camels, dogs, and horses, frightened Anna May and Ned. But Amy seemed comfortable with them. She put her trunk on the horses' faces, and the trained dogs ran under her belly. The noise of the city bothered Anna May. But Amy rose above the horn-honking and sirens and claxons, and one day with utter calm, she followed Buckles up the sidewalk of Amsterdam Avenue from Lincoln Center to the Sixty-seventh Street studios of ABC Television. After a ride in ABC's freight elevator, she walked down a hall, pausing to snag a muffin and quickly, an apple and orange, off the trolley outside the Green Room, where the other guests of the Kathy Lee Gifford and Regis Philbin show waited to appear.

The show's hosts greeted her with aahs, but Amy seemed unimpressed. She went into her routine before the TV cameras and then exited left, like one who had done it a hundred times before. In fact she *was* a celebrity, who had posed many times with movie stars such as Tom Cruise and Nicole Kidman, Dustin Hoffman, Geena Davis, Susan Sarandon, and Harrison Ford. They smiled at her as if genuinely awed by her size and grandeur, without knowing anything at all about her amazing story.

She was the mellowest of elephants. Nothing, Buckles said, fazed her. Blind children visited her after special circus performances and laughed as they crawled under her and swept their hands over the rough skin of her trunk. She frisked them for treats and nudged them aside, one after another. Amy clearly liked all kinds of people. She did not seem to have a "privacy" zone around her like most elephants, and she never seemed to mind when people came up to her and petted her trunk. She was accepting and agreeable, and always gentle.

But—only to be expected—there were days when she was as miserable as everyone else in the circus. If the audience did not applaud enough, she gave a lackluster performance. But when they cheered to her level of expectation she rewarded them, Buckles believed, with a smile. In the circus business, as Buckles was fond of pointing out, everyone, even the elephants, "got the bitter with the sweet."

CHAPTER ELEVEN

Bob buttonholed friends and acquaintances, business associates, new ranch hands, store cashiers, and sales assistants with tales of Amy's success in the circus. He showed off her "publicity" photographs. But always, behind his pride, he missed her sorely. He had stayed away, intentionally not visiting, to give her time to adjust to the circus world. He wanted her to forget him for her own good. "I guess that's what I was hoping for," he told Buckles. "But it still hurts a little."

"She seems pretty happy. I'll say that."

"It was a close call for a while, wasn't it?"

"I still can't tell you why she snapped out of it. Maybe it was a whole number of different things. Anna May was a big help. That's all far behind her now."

"When do you think I can come visiting?"

"Anytime," Buckles replied enthusiastically. "You'll be surprised how she's changed."

Yes, and that's what Bob was afraid of. He went from wondering if she missed him to the fear that she wouldn't remember him. He hadn't seen her in more than a year, during which she had lived through a major depression and had found a new life as the center of attention in a circus. He had only himself to blame if she had forgotten him, but he still felt guilty for letting her go.

He and Jane lived differently now, with Amy gone. Bob was competing in cutting horse competitions all over the West. He attended horse and cattle sales. He was elected the thirty-second president of the *American Quarter Horse Association* in Amarillo, Texas, and was inducted into its Hall of Fame. He helped to create the *National Cowboy Hall of Fame and Western Heritage Center* in Oklahoma City, and sat on its board of directors. He was a devoted father and grandfather. Most of these things he had postponed until now, because of Amy.

But the price he had not expected to pay for his freedom was that she would not know him anymore.

Before leaving home to take a flight back east, on the way to the airport Bob stopped at El Chorro's to pick up a bag of fresh sticky buns to bring to Amy, along with carrots and fresh strawberries dipped in chocolate On the airplane he wore his finest cowboy hat, his tooled cowhide boots, and his gold-worked prize belt buckle.

"Why, Bob, you look nervous," Jane observed wryly, as

they were leaving the motel in the town of Great Barrington, Massachusetts, where Amy was performing.

"I *am*—I'm goin' to see my gal."

Prepared for her not knowing him, he grew quiet and pensive as they drove within sight of the big top.

Buckles had seen to it that tickets were waiting at the booth. Bob looked around before entering the tent. The organization and size of the circus impressed him. He wondered where Buckles and the elephants were quartered. For a moment he listened, hoping to hear Amy's trumpeting welcome. Yes, he thought sadly, she has forgotten me.

All around the tent, open-sided caravans sold candy, souvenirs, and hot dogs; the air smelled of cotton candy, candy apples, popcorn, and soda, as well as the odor of the circus animals in their corrals and barns. Inside the tent a brass band was tuning up. A voice over a public-address system announced that the show was about to begin, and the members of the audience quickly filed in in the dim light to find their seats.

The tent covered a single ring. From their reserved folding chairs in the front row, on an aisle at the knee-high barrier that formed the center ring, Bob could reach his arm out into the ring itself. He *was* nervous. He looked over at a heavy curtain, where the performers entered and exited. He glanced down at his souvenir program, looking for the order of the performances. In his lap he held the bag of sticky buns and the carrots.

He felt like a "stage mother" when her child is about to

perform before a glittering audience. He wondered how much Amy had grown and changed; he still thought of her as a baby, barely bigger than a grown-up dog. The first time he had laid eyes on her seemed lifetimes ago. He was curious to see what more she had learned as a skilled "performer"? When she left the ranch, she knew the basics, and she had thrilled the schoolkids, as an indication of her talents. He wanted her to do well now, whatever she did with the circus act. He expected greatness of her, and he hoped he was not going to be disappointed.

The band started to play; the lights went down. The curtain parted. The human performers paraded in, one by one in single file, and walked around the ring styling and bowing, blowing kisses, greeting the audience in typical circus fashion, the clowns clowning, the acrobats tumbling, and a ringmaster—a white-haired older man in a white tailcoat—waving a black top hat, his other arm glittering with pastel parakeets on his sleeve. Bello Nock, his hair standing straight up, tripped, fell, and brushed himself off. The children seated behind Bob and Jane screamed out loud as a woman in a costume of bright sequins brought out trained dogs that jumped and tumbled in the air.

Then the curtain opened wide: Anna May entered. The audience cheered more loudly than before; Ned came out next; he was holding onto Anna May's tail. Then came Amy.

Bob sat up straight and stared. She *was* bigger. She *had* changed. She seemed mature. Poised. She had been so sad when they said good-bye. Her long eyelashes and brown eyes looked beautiful. She had never flared her ears as proudly for him as she did for the audience now. Oh, how he wanted to stand up and call out her name! He looked at Jane, who smiled at him knowingly, and she held his hand in hers.

The band quickened its tempo, and Bob slid to the edge of his chair. He leaned forward, waiting for Amy to come around to his side of the ring.

"Do you think she'll remember you?" Jane asked.

Bob was looking through the dark. "I guess probably not," he replied. If she had remembered him she would already have given a sign.

At that moment Amy dropped Ned's tail. She raised her trunk, as if she were searching the air. She trumpeted a sharp blast that startled the performers: Amy turned toward Bob. Through the dim light she stared across the ring. She held her trunk in the air like a question mark. Buckles, standing beside Anna May in his costume with the golden epaulets and the jodhpurs, scolded Amy under his breath. He had no idea what she was up to, but she was breaking the routine and that was not good.

"Amy! Move up!" he told her sternly.

She turned her head sideways, ignoring him, and then she broke ranks.

Buckles shouted, "Amy! Come here, Amy! Amy!"

She walked two, three steps to the center of the ring, and then she ran.

Buckles thought, Oh, God! She's rampaging!

She was trumpeting loudly and stopped in front of where Bob was sitting in the dark. He stood up, and the bag of sticky buns fell to the floor. He called out softly, "Amy!" She stepped up onto the knee-high barrier.

The whole performance came to an abrupt standstill. Collectively, all the people under the big top held their breath. Amy stepped over the low barrier into the aisle. She sank on her knees and laid her head in Bob's lap. She touched the tip of her trunk under his chin and all over his face. She made the chirrupping sound she had always made when she was happy.

"Good girl," Bob told her, choking with emotion. "Good Amy."

With her head still in his lap, she opened her mouth. He petted her tongue, as they used to do, and a soft purring sound came from deep in her throat.

The people in the audience recovered from their surprise. Still confused about what exactly they were witnessing, they sensed the presence of something special. Spontaneously they applauded.

Bob turned to Jane. "She *remembers* me," he said, with tears welling in his eyes.

He had stayed in Amy's heart. She would stay in his forever. She would never leave him, nor he leave her, in the permanent ways of the heart.

EPILOGUE

Circus people live partly in a make-believe world of brightly colored lights among the fictions of the show—artifice, illusions, and dreams. If they try hard they can even convince themselves that they are ageless, just as long as the show goes on. Buckles and Barbara had devoted their lives to this dream, but now change was coming to their world, overturning everything that they had ever known to be true.

In the winter of 1999 two incidents forced Buckles to wonder out loud to Barbara how elephants had lasted this long in the circus. "In the old days, they were its backbone. Today they're just a liability." And that meant Ned, Anna May, and Amy.

In the first incident two women protesters from a radical animal liberation group backed a dump truck up onto the sidewalk on Amsterdam Avenue, at the rear entrance to Lincoln Center, where the Big Apple was performing under its own big-top tent. In the rearest enclosure to their dump truck, on the other side of an iron fence, Amy, Anna May, and Ned were keeping warm in the elephant barn. It was a bitterly cold winter afternoon. The women dumped thousands of rotten apples out of the truck onto the sidewalk and then, quickly, before the police arrived, they put out signs reading: THE BIG APPLE IS ROTTEN TO ITS ANIMALS.

In the second disturbing incident that same winter, the Big Apple was camped in a field outside Princeton Junction, New Jersey, and its performers, handlers, and their animals were asleep. Suddenly an explosion lit up the sky. The main tent, the wagons, and the trailers all seemed to be ablaze. Two circus workers asleep in a trailer barely escaped the flames. The next morning the fire marshal found the shards of a Molotov cocktail. Another animal liberation group that cited the captivity of Amy, Anna May, and Ned as their cause claimed the "credit."

The Woodcocks—indeed, the whole Big Apple Circus— reacted with concern. Buckles told Barbara, "I can't imagine us continuing on. Elephants in circuses have become politically incorrect, that's all."

"The people from these groups would rather see our elephants dead," Barbara said angrily. "You can't tell them the truth, because they won't listen. There's no place with a waterfall and a unicorn where these creatures can go."

"The issue won't go away," said Buckles. "It's not just our elephants, it's the principle of the thing."

No one had ever cared more for elephants than Barbara
Woodcock. They were her "kids," and she had lived for
almost thirty years within easy calling of Anna May and,
more recently, of Amy and Ned. But now, she was forced by
her health to be satisfied with their images in her RV.

Back in 1979, when she was with Ringling Bros. Circus
World in Florida, she was riding atop an elephant, a leopard
beside her in a howdah—a large elephant saddle invented
by the Indians long ago. She entered the darkened ring.
Buckles was walking beside the elephant. A child in the
audience snapped a flash camera, and the startled elephant
jerked away. Barbara lost her balance and fell. The leopard
came down on top of her. The audience thought she was
being attacked. Barbara says, "He was licking me. He was
worried for me." The base of her spine had hit a board on
the ground, and she had fractured her bottom vertebra and
ruptured a disc. A sliver of bone had pierced the nerves in
her spine. From then on, when she was performing, jumping off horses, running and riding elephants, every time the
sliver moved Barbara went numb with pain.

Now, years later, she lived with morphine. This once-
vivacious woman who had danced on the backs of elephants
could hardly walk anymore. And she spent her days in remi-
niscence: "When I hear the circus music coming through the
trailer windows I sometimes start to cry," she said. "I was in
the ring before I could walk. I was an introvert who created

this outlandish person who danced and performed with animals. I just made the person up. And when I had to stop because of the pain, I didn't know which person I was—the introvert or the outlandish one."

She asked Buckles one day, "Who would take care of the elephants if you couldn't go on?"

Buckles didn't answer her. A complex dilemma faced him. What if something *did* happen to him? Not just anyone could take his place as the elephants' custodian, disciplinarian, and show master. With each passing year Amy and Ned, now preteenagers, needed more of about everything. Ned was big, rambunctious, and stubborn. Amy was maturing, and soon she would be ready to mate. Their constant bickering often led to fights. Who but Buckles could stop them?

Each day before sunrise Buckles got out of bed to feed them. He was often working in their barn late at night. He cleaned the stalls four times a day and exercised the elephants, watered them, and worked with them. Their grocery bill, which he paid out of his own purse—for fifty bales of hay, four bags of monkey biscuits, and carrots for treats each week—amounted to $407 and grew with the elephants.

Worst of all Buckles never stopped worrying that the elephants might hurt someone by accident. He had liability insurance, but that wasn't what bothered him. The circus audiences thought of the elephants as real-life Dumbos, but they were wild animals. One day in a moment of exhaustion he told Barbara, "I'd just like to get where I could stay home and not worry about somebody getting hurt."

"Well, what are you suggesting?" she asked.

"I don't know," he replied. "I don't know what's going to happen to us. But I do know that everything has to come to an end."

In Colorado, Bob was aware of Buckles's dilemma through conversations with Maguire. Bob weighed his interest in Amy's future welfare against his reluctance to interfere in another man's personal affairs. One evening, thinking about what would happen to Amy if Buckles decided to retire from the circus, he heard about a possible solution. As he had earlier when he was looking for a home for Amy, he tried to find out more about an unusual younger man named Randall Moore.

On a snowy night long ago, Randall Moore arrived as a stranger at an exotic animal farm in southern Washington. Moore's first thought was, This is a good place to hide out. At the time, as a college dropout with no aim in life, he was trying to avoid the U.S. Selective Service and the certainty, as he saw it then, of being sent to die in an unpopular war in Vietnam.

He offered his services, such as they were, to the owner of the farm. He had enthusiasm and energy, and not much else. But the owner of the farm hired him anyway. Few young men his age had the desire to handle wild animals. Even so, though the animals were exotic, the job was hardly glamorous, and the pay meager. Moore mucked out the stalls and fed and managed Phil, the lion; Joe, his cage mate; André, a Russian brown bear; his mate, Sonja, and Tanja, their baby; the hybrid bears Natasha and Sasha; five performing Asian bull elephants billed as "the Tuskers of Thailand," and three African elephants—Durga, Owalla, and Tshombe, orphans like Amy from a cull.

Tshombe was a big bull, fifteen years old, headstrong and independent, with handsome tusks. Owalla, a teenager, was the trio's matriarch, with a strong will and the inclination to use force to instill discipline; Durga, a submissive and docile younger female with cherubic features and long eyelashes, just wanted to get along.

Moore studied their traits and saw a reasonable reflection of himself. As African elephants they were a misunderstood species. He felt the same about himself. The African elephants had a reputation for being unmanageable. Moore's parents thought of him that way and had told him so. The elephants were stubborn; Moore's teachers had chosen to use the word "intractable" to describe him. The elephants were endangered as a species, and if the army caught him, that was what Moore would be.

The owner of the farm, Morgan Berry, an older man with a twinkle in his eye and a colorful past, loved to tell Moore stories about strange animal happenings in some of the far-flung places he had visited in his lifetime. At the kitchen table one night, he described a place in the former Belgian Congo (now Democratic Republic of Congo) called Gangala-na-Bodio, where captured African elephants long ago were trained to pull plows and clear the land of mahogany trees.

"*African* elephants?" asked Moore. "I thought they couldn't be trained."

"Apparently those rumors are wrong."

"Then what about Owalla, Durga, and Tshombe?"

"Why don't you see what you can do with them?" Berry replied with a challenge his young employee was quick to take up.

Of the three African elephants, Owalla was fast to learn, Tshombe needed constant reassurance, and Durga was unsure and slow. Over the winter months of training—as he taught them to perform simple exercises—Moore formed an emotional attachment to them. As the year progressed, he decided that circus tricks diminished their majesty, and embraced a strange commitment for their future together: It was right and principled for them to go back to where they were born. And he, Randall Moore, would take them there.

It was a dream he kept to himself in the year that he, with Morgan Berry and Berry's companion, an animal trainer named Eloise Berchtold, took their animal acts on the road. Eloise trained Berry's Asian elephants, performing with them as part of the Rudi Brothers Circus. The life fascinated Moore for a short time, but finally he decided that it wasn't for him. The draft was no longer a worry once the lottery was introduced, and he received a high number that surely would keep him safe. Now, with his newfound freedom, he wanted to continue to work with elephants as an anthropologist, and for that he was going to need an advanced formal education.

He left Berry's employ in the mid-seventies to enroll in Florida's Santa Fe Teaching Zoo, working at nights as a hotel maintenance man and a lab technician to pay the tuition. He quickly learned the philosophy and ethics of animal conservation. He discovered how the destiny of humankind was linked with that of its fellow creatures. He read every book in the library about African elephants and, to satisfy his curiosity about Africa itself, he found other books like Isak Dinesen's *Out of Africa*, which filled him with the romantic desire someday to explore that part of the world. He was restless to begin with. He never stayed with one thing for long. Soon he dropped out of the teaching zoo to join a project in Mexico studying an endangered species of turtle.

When Morgan Berry was killed by one of his own Asian elephants, a bull named Buddha, Moore flew to his farm to take over the care of the animals. Berry's lawyer and the executor of his estate greeted him with an offer to sell him the farm and its animals.

"I can't afford that," Moore told him when he heard the price. "I can't afford *anything*. But I'm the only one who knows these animals."

"Then the animals will be sold off to zoos," he was told.

"Not zoos or circuses, please!"

"Then where else?"

"I don't know. I just want something positive to happen to them," Moore said. "I want to take Owalla, Tshombe, and Durga back to Africa."

"On what?" He asked fifty thousand dollars for the three.

"I don't have anywhere near that much," Moore told him. "Anyway, wouldn't it be like taking coals to Newcastle?"

"I'm not talking about *all* elephants. This is about these three. I know them. They are my friends. They are orphans, and I don't want them to go to a zoo or a circus." He thought, This is a chance for all of us, the elephants *and* me. Make up your mind. Right now, for once, *finish* what you started. Get them back to Africa and set them free!

"Let me see what I can do," he told the attorney.

"You've got two weeks," was his reply. "Then they go to the highest bidder."

Working out of a phone booth, Moore called a magazine editor he knew in New York City, who referred him to the producer of a television program on ABC called *The American Sportsman*. Moore pitched his idea over the phone. After a lengthy silence, the producer asked, "You're serious?"

"Yes, sir, I am."

"You want me to ask Roone Arledge to buy three elephants and ship them to Africa? You must be crazy." At the time Arledge was the head of ABC Sports.

"That is what I'm asking, yes, sir," Moore replied.

"Well, it might be nuts enough to be a good idea. I need a show."

"I need a sponsor."

The producer paused, thinking back. The previous summer he had been sitting around a campfire in the wilds of Kenya with a naturalist, a photographer, and a tourist camp operator, who had wondered out loud, "Wouldn't it be neat to get elephants out here to ride around on and view the wild animals?"

"It sure would make a good show," the producer had said. And the idea stayed in his mind ever since.

"What do you say?" Moore asked him.

"Let's do it!" he told Moore.

He offered him a two-year contract, the cost of Berry's three African elephants, and all expenses paid.

With a newly minted *American Sportsman* credit card, Moore bought shovels, brooms, and bales of hay and rented a semi to drive the elephants to a cattle ranch near Tampico, Mexico, that he was offered for free as a staging base for the sea voyage back to Africa. Owalla, Tshombe and Durga had to learn how to carry men on their backs, as Moore saw it, as a necessary skill that would help him to reintroduce them into the African wilds. Moore was learning himself by trial and error, sticking to a singular dictum: "Infinite patience, skill, and a certain degree of insanity will get me by."

On the appointed day, the cargo ship SS *Mormaclynx* left its pier on the East River in Brooklyn with a supercargo of three elephants in open-topped steel containers. In his suitcase Moore carried visas, medical reports, entry permits, and the promise of high government officials to let him and his elephants enter Kenya, on Africa's east coast. The thirty-six-day voyage around the Cape of Good Hope began in New York Harbor with the sight of the Statue of Liberty and the promise for Moore of a dream come true.

One day out of Cape Town, South Africa, a pod of seven short-finned pilot whales broke the surface in rolling seas. They spouted and raced beside the ship in clear sight of the elephants on deck. Excitedly the elephants extended their trunks over the rail and called out with guttural sounds. As one of the whales rose up on a wave and came nearly within the reach of the elephants' trunks, Owalla let rip a trumpet blast that convinced Moore: These two endangered species were actually *talking*.

Finally, when they tied up to the dock at the Kenyan port of Mombasa, a minister of the Kenyan government met the ship. He was carrying a walking stick carved out of elephant ivory and wore an ivory bracelet on his wrist. Armed guards joined him on the ship's gangway, and with the first words out of his mouth, he demanded a bribe—or else the elephants would not disembark on Kenyan soil.

"This is a bad beginning," Moore told him.

"Then you will go back home."

"But home is eight thousand miles from here."

At last, after hasty transatlantic phone calls, the elephants were allowed to step off the ship but remained under virtual house arrest on the edge of Tsavo Game Park. Over the next four months, while Moore begged the government to honor its agreement, and while he was starting to introduce the elephants back into the wild, Tshombe, the stubborn bull with the handsome tusks, contracted salmonella from stagnant water and died.

The death came as a terrible blow to Moore. He remembers, "Tshombe's death hit me hard, and it was to be a long time before I overcame my grief. I had spent more time with Tshombe than the other two, having ridden him for hours on end in the bush. It had been a relationship of deep mutual respect and, dare I say it, affection. In that period of mourning I recalled an amazing incident on board the ship which had brought us to Africa. I had been standing on the deck gazing idly to sea, when I felt an elephant's trunk wrapping itself around my waist and, very gently, pulling me. It was Tshombe. He pulled me right up to his chest and held me firmly in his trunk. . . . There was no doubt it was a show of affection. It was one of the most gratifying moments of my elephant experience, and recollection of it made Tshombe's death that much more agonizing."

Now, after all his good intentions, all this effort, he wondered what had he done that, in the end, was positive? He buried Tshombe, and he waited to know whether the government would allow him to remain in Kenya long enough to reintroduce Owalla and Durga back into the wild. The answer came. He was to be expelled, with Owalla and Durga. He was not to come back.

"Why?" Moore asked one sympathetic member of the Kenyan parliament whose efforts on his behalf had failed.

"Officially I do not know. Unofficially it's because your elephants are South African elephants."

"What are you talking about?"

"Not me, but the minister you refused the bribe. Your elephants were born in South Africa. According to him they are not good for Kenya."

Moore looked incredulous. "Nothing will ever surprise me again," he said, as he prepared for the sea journey that took him and his charges down the east coast of Africa. He thought sardonically, *Out of Africa*? This is more like *The Rime of the Ancient Mariner*.

But when the ship arrived in South Africa, port officials ordered him to keep the elephants on board and keep sailing, citing a threat of the spread of hoof-and-mouth disease.

"But elephants don't carry that disease," Moore pointed out to them. "What's the threat?"

"One-year quarantine in a country without hoof-and-mouth disease, then you can bring them back in."

"Where?"

"There are several countries to choose from. The United States for one."

"I came from there."

"Then you know the way back."

He was finally beginning to understand why no one had ever tried to bring an African elephant back to Africa before.

After a year with the elephants in quarantine outside Washington, D.C., the South African ambassador to the United States agreed to help Moore if he would stop his badgering. The *American Sportsman* renewed its sponsorship, and finally, with a clean bill of health, Durga and Owalla boarded yet another freighter. By now, Moore had traveled thirty thousand miles together with his outcasts. He was personally running out of steam. He had one last chance, and this time he got lucky. With their own yearnings to be free of apartheid, the black people of South Africa greeted Owalla and Durga as returned prodigals.

Moore planned to release the elephants back in the wild on a game preserve in Pilanesberg, where rangers were searching for surrogate mother elephants for orphaned bulls that were running out of control. About to try what no one had done before, Moore rode his elephants on the reserve, and soon they were feeding off natural vegetation and drinking from streams and lakes, after years in captivity, eating baled hay and drinking fluoridated water out of the end of a hose. One evening as he was riding Owalla, they came upon a waterhole, and suddenly Durga's ears flared and she let out a scream. A large female white rhino with a young calf at her side was standing there. "Steady, steady,"

Moore told Owalla. With her head down, ears flared, and trumpeting loudly Durga charged the rhinos. Moore followed on Owalla, and as they broke through a growth of acacias, Moore saw that Durga was still trumpeting loudly. In the distance the rhino and her baby were running out of sight.

Moore praised his elephants lavishly for overcoming their nervousness. They had stood up to the only animal in Pilanesberg that had the weight and power to threaten them.

Slowly, day by day, he gave his elephants more freedom, until they were allowed to wander on their own without him on their backs. Every night they returned to camp, and every morning they set out again to explore the wild. The seasonal rains came and went; then one day the elephants did not return.

Moore went out to search for them, fearing that they had been shot by poachers. Just before dark he thought that he heard an elephant call, but he wasn't sure. He looked over a small, secluded valley. He strained his ears at the silence, certain that his imagination had played tricks. Then he heard the sound again. He focused on the far horizon: There, Durga, Owalla, and three wild orphaned bulls were grazing peacefully in the tall grass.

Owalla looked in Moore's direction, as if waiting for his command. Moore thought, There won't be one. This is our final parting.

And with that the elephants vanished in the dusk.

For once, Moore had finished something he had begun. The newness of the experience changed him. He said to himself, to his own surprise, *You did something that nobody has ever done. Why quit now?*

He returned to the United States for more captive elephants that he would take home. He found a majestic, handsome bull elephant named Abu locked in a farmer's barn, lying on a concrete floor in the dark with his feces caked on the sides of his head. Somehow, his owner had avoided the protective vigilance of the USDA. Moore bought him on the spot with funds that he had raised for that purpose in South Africa after the success of his initial experiment. The Fort Worth Zoo gave him an unwanted, floppy-eared and very forlorn African elephant named Benny. It had one broken tusk and another that was worn to a nub from rubbing against his cage. Last, Moore bought two African orphans named Cathy and Sammy from a safari park near Toronto. Sammy was neglected and for a time had even broken pond ice with his tusks for fresh water to drink. Cathy was a strong leader, Moore said, with the sweet look of a cherub.

With high hopes he booked this new brood on a freighter leaving from Savannah. He banked on his previous experiences in South Africa, when his elephants were greeted in the press and public with enthusiasm, but when the ship finally reached the port at Durban, South Africa, no crowd and no press were waiting. The novelty of African elephants being returned to their original homes had clearly worn off. Again Moore was on his own.

With the help of a patron in the tourism business, he conceived of an idea to create a "halfway house" for African elephants between captivity and freedom in the wild. The first time around, he had taught Owalla and Durga to carry humans on their backs. That led him now to ask himself, Why not teach these new elephants to carry tourists, as they are adjusting to the wild? The directors of an ecotourism company welcomed his idea and agreed to a ten-week trial on a large track of wilderness in Botswana, north of South Africa.

Moore rode his elephants more than two hundred miles in eight days, crossing the Kalahari Desert into an African wilderness of pelicans, storks, and cranes, myriad geese, ducks, and hundreds of different bush birds. The elephants fed on varieties of new vegetation and traveled through herds of plains game—zebras, buffalo, giraffes, impalas, tssesebe, and lechwe (antelopes), and reedbucks. Finally, they reached the site of the Okavango Delta, which the guidebooks refer to as "The Last Eden."

Moore pitched a tent on the shore of a lagoon and christened the camp "Abu's."

To be certain about Randall Moore, Bob called Maguire to ask him if he knew anything about him.

Maguire said, "I know about what he's done over there."

"What would you recommend? Is it a good place for Amy?"

"*Definitely*," Maguire replied.

And that was all that Bob needed to hear.

Buckles had wanted Bob to decide what to do with Amy. After all, by his thinking, she was still Bob's elephant. But with time and schedules, the pressure was mounting. For one thing the circus had announced Buckles's retirement at the end of summer 2000, a date that was fast approaching. He thought he had found a place for Ned with Ringling's circus, and Anna May was retiring with him and Barbara to Florida. He supposed that a circus or a zoo would buy Amy, but he was uncertain what to do.

Then one night when the Big Apple Circus was performing at its home site at Lincoln Center, the cell phone rang in the RV, and Buckles picked it up. He listened to a voice from far away that sounded, he said, like something whispered through a long tunnel.

"My name is Randall Moore," the caller said.

"I've heard of you," Buckles told him. He quickly had to remind himself: Moore had taken some elephants back to Africa. At the time he thought the story sounded bizarre. No one took elephants *back* to Africa. Why would anyone bother to send them back only to have them shot? It made no sense to him.

For a while the two men, an ocean apart, talked about elephants and elephant people in common. They traded the names of elephants as other men and women bandy those of college classmates and friends. *Flora was where? How was she doing these days? And the big bull, Tembo? He was in Munich. What about Matadi and Jimmy?* Moore asked pointedly about Anna May, knowing how much she meant to Buckles.

Then, as Buckles was starting to wonder about the purpose of his call, Moore said, "I've been hearing reports on your Amy."

"You have?" said Buckles. "Just what have you heard, Mr. Moore?"

"That you're looking for someone to take good care of her."

"Maybe that's true. What do you have in mind?"

"I'd like to bring her over here to where she started," Moore said. "I'm looking for Africans like her. I'll bring 'em all back if I can. She has had an odyssey from what I hear. She deserves the best."

"Well, I'll be darned," Buckles said.

AFTERWORD

ate had chosen Amy to live while her family died. It carried her into a strange human world that few elephants had known before. She did what she had to do in her new world, and more. No one can ever say what made her different. She was "mellow" and learned human ways. Her curiosity seemed to quell any "anger" or "resentment," or any of the other feelings that could have come naturally to her. She behaved like a "lady." She was gentle and sweet, held herself with a kind of dignity, and innately seemed to understand that she was different. The description of her itself as merely a survivor insulted the success of her effort. A brightness from within had seemed to guide her and keep her safe, and that, finally, was all that anyone could say.

When she reached the Woodcocks' farm in Florida at the

start of Buckles's and Barbara's retirement, Ned had gone to another circus, and Anna May, out in the fields of palmettos and green grass, simply settled down and relaxed after forty years of work.

Amy was reaching an age when hormonal yearnings were calling to her. She had babies to give birth to, a family to raise, a herd to adopt and travel with, and middle age and old age to reach among her own kind. She would reach these stages of her life in Africa, where she would be returning.

She certainly had a story to tell the wild elephants of Africa. But what would it really say? Probably simple truths: Life was worth living, her story could begin. People, *species*, races, and ages were pretty much the same everywhere—meaning, there were good and there were bad. You had the power to choose your part in the drama of your own life. If you chose good, more often than not your life would be a happy one.

What a *beautiful* story that was for the Storyteller to tell back in Africa!

Bob rides a different horse these days. This stallion— young, frisky, and able to travel the fence lines for miles without tiring—was not even born when Amy, Bob, Big Bob, Butch, and Jo rode together. Bob feels good about everything that happened, though the certain knowledge that another chance like it will not come again naturally saddens him a little. An animal like Amy is a once-in-a-lifetime happening. He was lucky, he guesses, for that. He is old now, and there isn't as much trail in him left to ride. Looking back, his friendship with Amy shines like a star.

"She meant more to me than I can ever say," he says.

ACKNOWLEDGMENTS

Sometimes stories are just waiting to be found. This one about Bob and Amy appeared on a visit to my mother-in-law. An enlarged photograph lying on her kitchen counter showed a cowboy, his legs draped in chaps, on a horse, with what appeared to be a baby elephant standing horse-flank-high by his side. "Oh, that's my friend Bob Norris, and that's his elephant, Amy," my mother-in-law told me, sounding as if all her friends had an elephant in their yard.

I called Bob soon after, introduced myself, and asked him to tell me whether it was true that he had adopted an orphan elephant? His voice over the telephone at first conjured up images of the Old West. As he confirmed the facts, I formed the impression of a nonconformist who was a symbol of a unique and disappearing part of the American experience. Indeed, he said, the story of him and Amy was every bit true.

I thought that others might share my curiosity about this odd and unlikely relationship. I put the idea in the able hands of Michael Carlisle of the literary agency Carlisle & Co., who has shepherded into print interesting and different stories, like those of the giraffe *Zarafa* by Michael Allin and *Longitude* by Dava Sobel. Thomas Dunne and Peter Wolverton, editors at St. Martin's Press and Thomas Dunne Books, both had the imagination to see this story as a book before it was written.

To begin with, I traveled several times for long durations out to Colorado and Nevada to be with Bob and Jane and their ranch hands at T Cross. Bob gave generously of his time and patience and relived to the best of his ability his days with Amy. Buckles and Barbara Woodcock allowed me to tag along with them and the Big Apple Circus, and Buckles's companionship and the oral history of the circus he carries around in his head provided for many pleasurable and informative days. The Big Apple's management, especially Paul Binder and Gary Dunning, gave me all the access to their circus that I could have wished.

On a research trip to Africa, Randall Moore showed me parts of the continent I'd not visited before. I had lived in Nairobi, Kenya, for three years in the 1970s as a correspondent for *Newsweek* magazine and in the early 1980s as a book writer. In those days I traveled more or less continuously

ACKNOWLEDGMENTS

over black Africa on assignment, often trying to find occasions to observe elephants, which have fascinated me for a very long time. I did not ever study elephants in those years in Africa—far from it. I observed them as anyone would, and I listened to the people who did study them, hunt them, and live among them.

In my research for this book, Randall Moore loaned me a tent at his Abu's Camp in the Okavango Delta of Botswana. I observed his elephants up close. I also watched other wild elephants in Botswana. Those observations helped to bring me up-to-date. I drew quite a bit of knowledge from long conversations with Moore, his mahouts, and with hunters around the campfire. Moore's expertise and long history with elephants were especially valuable.

In Zimbabwe, Buck and Rita deVries were my generous hosts on their farm in the Gwayi Valley. Buck introduced me to Siwelo Bvathlomoy Dingani and some of the neighboring Tonga tribesmen. Buck shared a wealth of knowledge about elephants, the cull, and about Amy's early years. His kindness and generosity toward me will be long remembered. He introduced me to elephant and other animal researchers in his area, and to officials in Zimbabwe's Game Department who carried out the culls that orphaned Amy. They helped me to put together a fairly accurate picture of Amy's family and its last days.

Last, I hung around with Amy. She was always a pleasure to watch, to sit with, and interact with. She is a remarkable creature. She has a great future to look forward to in Botswana, where she will stay at Abu's Camp until she can be released into the wild.

I would especially like to thank the travel company Abercrombie & Kent, Oak Park, Illinois—Christa Bradsch, Rosemary Kinyanjui of the Abercrombie & Kent Global Foundation, and Mrs. Jorie Butler Kent—for their spirited cooperation and their kindness toward Amy.

As always I owe my love and everlasting appreciation to my wife, Charlie, who believed in the goodness of this tale from the very start and kept the book on track, as she usually does with the author—with humor, tolerance, and love.

MORE ABOUT ELEPHANTS

Bazé, W. *Just Elephants*. London: Elek books, 1955.

Bell, W. D. M. *Karamojo Safari*. London: Safari Press, 1989.

Blunt, D. E. *Elephant*. Suffolk, UK: Major Books, 1933.

Campbell, R. *Elephant King*. New York: Junior Literary Guild, 1931.

Cooper, C. R. *Boss Elephant*. Boston: Little, Brown, 1939.

Echlin, Kim. *Elephant Winter*. New York: Carroll & Graf, 1990.

Fletcher, S. E. *The Cowboy and His Horse*. New York: Grosset & Dunlap, 1951.

Masson, J. M. and S. McCarthy. *When Elephants Weep*. New York: Delacorte Press, 1995.

Moore, Randall. *Back to Africa*. Cape Town: Southern Book Publishers, 1989.

Moss, C. *Portraits in the Wild: Behavior Studies of East African Mammals*. Chicago: University of Chicago Press, 1982.

Payne, Katy. *Silent Thunder: In the Presence of Elephants*. New York: Simon & Schuster, 1998.

Petzinger, T., Jr. *Oil and Honor*. New York: G. P. Putnam's Sons, 1987.

Poole, Joyce. *Coming of Age with Elephants*. New York: Hyperion, 1996.

Sanderson, I. T. *The Dynasty of Abu*. New York: Knopf, 1962.

Sillar, F. C., and R.M. Meyler. *Elephants: Ancient and Modern*. New York: Viking, 1968.

Smith, E. C. *Kongo the Elephant*. New York: Knopf, 1939.

Symons, R. D. *Where the Wagon Led*. New York: Doubleday, 1973.

Szechenyi, Z. *Land of Elephants*. New York: Putnam, 1935.

Ward, F. E. *The Working Cowboy's Manual*. New York: Bonanza Books, 1983.

White, E. L. *The Elephant Never Forgets*. London: Harper and Brothers, 1938.

Williams, J. H. *Elephant Bill*. New York: Doubleday, 1950.